I0568398

Fear
and
Love
Motivation

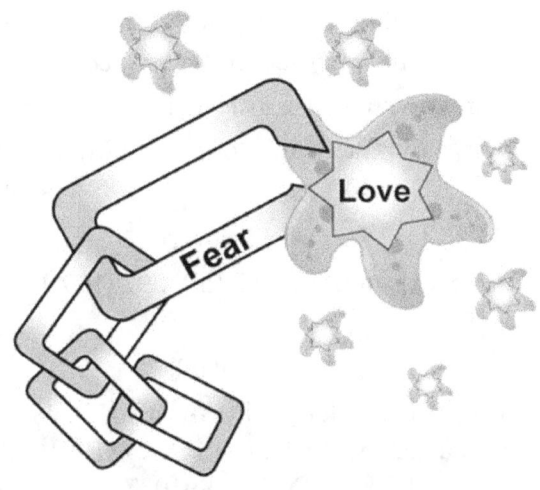

Self-Healing by Reclaiming the Power of Your Thoughts, Feelings, Words and Colours

Jansie Bond

Address all general enquiries to Jansie Bond:
Email: jansiebond@gmail.com
You can also contact Jansie via her Facebook page:
https://www.facebook.com/RainbowDivinity/

Second edition 2022
Paperback International: ISBN 9781991027283

Also available
Paperback print-on-demand USA: ISBN 9798356297557
Paperback New Zealand: ISBN 9781991027290
PDF: ISBN 9781991027306
ePub: ISBN 9781991027313

Philip Garside Publishing Ltd
PO Box 17160
Wellington 6147
New Zealand
books@pgpl.co.nz — www.pgpl.co.nz

Every attempt has been made to
properly attribute all quotes.

"All that we are is the result of what we have thought.
The mind is everything.
What we think we become."

— Buddha

Dedication

I dedicate this book to you, the Reader, who may be in various phases of awakening to the power of the Divine Love within you. It is my heartfelt wish that between the pages of this book you will find the inspiration to live a life that will inspire others.

This book is about awakening to the power of your thoughts, feelings, words, and actions. It is about ordinary people who do something every day to make the world a better place for themselves and those around them. In order to inspire others, we first have to find the greatness and love in ourselves.

While writing this book, I often felt like I was only typing the words that came through me from Spirit. Many times, I was filled with feelings of reverence for how my Spirit team woke me up every night for four months at all hours of the night to write while the house was sleeping. I sometimes had a quiet chuckle at the appropriate websites or books and quotes that I opened at exactly the right time — sources of information I needed so I could understand some of the wonderful messages my "Spirit Team" was conveying through me.

It is, therefore, with deep gratitude that I also dedicate this book to all my Teachers, those who are walking this Earth and the Divine Beings and Guides who have been with me on my life journey. Their unconditional love assisted me in waking up to the light within.

My journey took me through deep valleys of fear. The compassion and patience of my Teachers helped me find my truth in the darkness of a fear-filled life and change it to a life lived in love. With this book, I am passing that love on to you, the Reader.

We all get motivated through either fear or love. When we are afraid, we are alive but not living. Love lets us live with exuberance every moment. Our challenge is to learn self-love before we can spread love around. Changing your fear into love is the most important and best journey you can embark on.

I hope that once you have travelled your journey over the Rainbow and found the gold in your heart, together we will ignite the "flame of Love" all over the world.

Acknowledgements

To my husband, Weldon, thank you for your ongoing support and belief in me and for allowing me to find my own way in life. You have been my husband, teacher, lifelong friend, confidant, business partner, sounding board, editor, and my rock. You have taught me so much about living love.

To Anri, our daughter, your unwavering support on so many levels made it possible for me to write this book knowing that you are my rope holder. (The story of a rope holder is in Chapter 16.)

To Brian, our son, thank you for the numerous emails and affirmations you sent me. You were always quick to respond and come to my aid when I needed help.

To Schaldine, my other daughter, your sense of humour while I was going through hard patches writing this book made my heart sing with joy.

My father showed me how a man should treat his wife. My mother taught me to love words and how to write stories. They were the first people to welcome me into this world — and with much love, they created a safe place for me and my brother to spend a happy childhood. Their love and trust in my abilities carried me through my whole life. Mom and Dad, I miss you every day and I will love you forever.

Like a spiderweb glistening in the sunlight, I had a strong network of family, friends, and clients who formed a safe web for me. Without their support, phone calls, Facebook messages, emails, and visits, the lessons of my life would have been so much harder. Siobhan Cuff, Jenny House, Alida Idema, Renee van Zyl and Lynette Visagie, I thank you for forming the anchor points for my web.

To my book teachers — your books are on my shelves, but I carry your words and your teachings in my heart. You came to me in mysterious and miraculous ways. I salute you in gratitude.

A special word of thanks to:

Patrick Snow — you gave me the structure I needed to bring this book to life.

Tyler Tichelaar, who edited my book and helped me with the final product. Through your comments you showed me the warmth and humour of the person who could otherwise only have been a faceless teacher changing sentences and correcting punctuation.

Weldon Bond — thank you for the picture graphics in the book which clearly reflect my ME ROADMAP.

Photographer — Brian Sheppard you took a picture of me that even I like.

Cover and Layout — Blanche Price, I think of you with gratitude in my heart.

Publisher — Philip you were instrumental for my book to go worldwide. Gratitude fills my heart for your contribution to my book.

Contents

When the student becomes the teacher, the teacher smiles.

— Spirit

Preface — A Note to the Reader

Fear and Love Motivation is a book about learning first of all to love ourselves unconditionally using our fear as the starting point; it's about the power of the words we use, the healing properties of colour, and how we create our world with our thoughts and feelings. It is a book for anyone who wants to find inner power and to restore life from within.

I invite you to walk with me through the pages of my life in this book; hopefully, doing so will open you up to the wonder of your own life. I am aware that some of my statements may be controversial to some of my readers. Please don't stop reading if you get to a chapter or story that you cannot relate to or do not like. This book is meant for you to work through your own blocks, and the subconscious knows when the ego might need to change; in those situations, the ego will fight for its own survival, which can mean that you will put this book away instead of reading it to the end.

I love reading, but I do not just read a book. I study it and make notes as I work through it. I write the pages of my favourite parts in its front or back. I hope you will make this book your own by doing the same. I have given you the opportunity to write your story about fear and love motivation in your life at the end of each of my stories under the heading "write your own story." Please use your own book. Enjoy your journey with me. I hope you will find benefits and new ways to heal some of the patterns in your life that are preventing you from living a life of abundance on all levels.

Somewhere in this book you will find the gift, the moment of truth for you. It is a gift from the Divine to you. I serve only as its facilitator by writing this book. It is up to you to find your gift that can change your life to one in which you live, love, and experience abundance on all levels. It is a great revelation and a blessing when we know for certain that God speaks from within us, through us, to us, and for us.

In this book, you will read about "ME" and also "ME=EM." Everywhere I speak about "ME" in capital letters it means My Energy, and you can read it as your Energy. Please keep in mind that in the beginning of my self-healing journey, I started out with EM which meant Energy

Management. I soon realised the only energy I could manage was my own, and that is how I started to talk about "ME" meaning "my energy." I created this explanation, which I find a powerful affirmation myself, for ME=EM:

> *"The impact of My Energy is determined by my choices*
> *and how much effort I put into my Energy Management."*

The "roadmap" I use throughout the journey in this book is the result of these 4 letters. I created new words like "Frighters, Flighters, Fighters", "desert road", "Fear Bus", and "Love Bus", to name only a few. These words are in italics in the book. My business name is *Rainbow Divinity*, and I say we learn to speak *Rainbow Language*.

In order to protect people's privacy, I changed some names in my stories and blended different people's stories for their protection.

I like using quotes because they represent many years of wisdom and experience by the author who wrote the quote. I spent many hours and worked through hundreds of quotes to get the right quote for each particular story to illustrate how I felt. Many of the quotes do not have names with them, but I call those quotes "my unknown voice" because they were like my thoughts spoken by an unknown person, so it is with gratitude that I use them.

I do not claim to be an expert in any field. This is my version, about my experiences in my own life. The information in this book is no substitute for consulting a health care professional. All information contained in this book, including information relating to medical and health conditions, products, and treatments is for informational purposes only. Please see your doctor or health care professional before starting any alternative treatments, diets, supplements, or exercise programme.

Introduction — A Colourful Journey to Freedom

To write this book, I had to go back to the beginning of my journey. Doing so affected me on many levels. I remember a questionnaire I had to complete about my fear and stress levels many years ago. I start with this questionnaire to demonstrate to you the role colour played in my healing and that colour is now one of the pillars of my healing practice. The following questions I still use in my colour manual. Every question represents a different colour:

- Do you have enough money to do the things you want to do?
- Do you have weight problems like overeating or anorexia?
- Are you caught up in situations in your life where you feel powerless?
- Do you feel people are taking advantage of you at work or at home?
- Do you have difficulty with authority, and do you challenge the status quo?
- Do you find it difficult to switch off your mind and you over-analyse problems?

The above questions and many more are the ones I struggled with during certain periods of my life. I over-analysed my problems to such an extent that I suffered from depression. I suffered health problems for many years, and I know that physical pain can break down your defences. I have felt lonely and misunderstood for a long time.

The facilitator who gave me the questionnaire explained to me that according to my answers, the following could be true about my life: You are suffering from stress-related illnesses. You are in financial difficulties. You would like to change your job, but you are too afraid to leave. You cannot talk about situations that are out of control in your life. Due to all your problems, your relationships are not happy. You are often feeling depressed or that life is not worth living. At that stage of my life, the statements were all true.

In the years that followed, I learned how to recognise and work with those issues that stemmed from fear motivation. Throughout this book, I share my stories which you can use to heal your fears. You will learn how to assess your fear reactions, when confronted with challenging situations in your life. You will discover that you are motivated through fear or love, and you can choose how you react to life's challenges. You will learn techniques to conquer fear. We create our lives through our thoughts, feelings, and words; therefore, if we change the way we think, feel, and speak, we can change our circumstances.

On our journey through this book, we will look at the immense power of words and learn that many words have answers within them. I call the words and messages hiding within a word a *word reveal*. There can be more than one word hiding in the words, but I use the most relevant word(s) to remind us how we use words and the healing or hurting power of the word.

One of my favourite sayings is that the most basic need of every human being is to feel appreciated. The word reveal for "appreciates" gives me a whole sentence: "Repeat praise; it appeases peers." When I lived in South Africa, I helped companies implement recognition systems. In the word "recognition" is "ignite." It is a well-known fact that appreciation and recognition of people can ignite a flame not just in the individual, but also in any work environment. It is my sincere wish that in reading this book, you will realise that to recognise and appreciate the beauty in yourself can ignite a flame in your life that can change it forever.

You will be guided into the concept that everything is energy and when we accept that idea, how our lives can change. You will see that we are all influenced by colour every day, and with the knowledge of colour's healing power, which has been known and practiced for thousands of years, you can heal yourself.

Write down your own experiences in a separate book when you see the heading "write your own story." Actively participating you will change many of your outdated beliefs and harmful behaviour patterns.

I have personally lived the *roadmap* of *fear and love* for most of my life. I studied colour and have practiced as a qualified colour healing therapist for more than twenty years. I read and studied many books about motivation and self-healing. I taught courses on how to manage energy on a personal and corporate level in South Africa and now in New Zealand. I also teach colour courses, and have helped many people over the years through my healing modalities to understand and heal their own lives. I help people who are afraid of failure, because they think they are not good enough, to recognise and appreciate the beauty in themselves by building their self-confidence and self-love.

I know what it feels like to doubt yourself or feel that you will never be able to change your behaviour and break the patterns of repetition and negativity. I know that work and life happen to all of us; we get caught up in the challenges of everyday life and feel we do not have energy to change or try any new ideas.

I want you to know that I still experience low points in my life, but knowing how to deal with my fears, I now see them as stepping stones to learn how to love myself. I know a divine spark exists in all of us that keeps us trying to achieve our highest potential, no matter how many times we feel like giving up.

Come with me on a journey through this book. I want to share with you how I healed myself, and I would be honoured if you let me help you through the challenges in your own life.

Are you ready to take a ride on the *fear* and *love bus* with me? Are you prepared to bring your baggage of fear, pain, sadness, anger, stress, and loneliness? Would you like to exchange it for love, laughter, gratitude, peace, and happiness? Please join me as we get onboard our bus for a colourful journey to find freedom! I promise you that the destination will be worth your while and it can be the best journey you have ever taken.

Jansie Bond

"The Lord gave you a body that can stand most anything. It's your mind you have to convince."

— Vince Lombardi

Part I

Fear Motivation

"Fear doesn't exist anywhere except in the mind."
— Dale Carnegie

Chapter 1 — Learning Through Fear

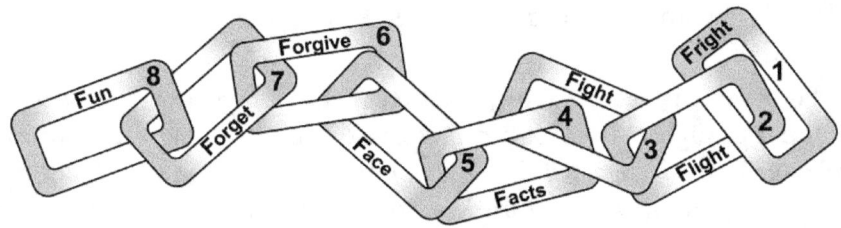

"Fear is the main source of superstition,
and one of the main sources of cruelty.
To conquer fear is the beginning of wisdom."
— Bertrand Russell

In this first chapter, we will look at the fact that we are born without fear and explore how our families, friends, teachers, and society motivate us through fear, although they all think they do it with love. I like the way Don Miguel Ruiz describes this phenomenon: "We are born without fear and then we get domesticated. Fear is like a virus on earth and it gets passed on to young children by their loving siblings, parents, teachers, friends and family."

If you skipped the Preface and Introduction, please read it before you start this chapter. In the Introduction, I mentioned the concept that *everything is energy, and when we accept that idea, how our lives can change.* If we think we are a Spirit in a human body, it makes sense to me that our Spirit needs a form to manifest and, therefore, our body is an important vehicle on Earth. Children are born without fear, so what happens to change us into fear-filled beings?

Fearing Darkness

Were you afraid of the dark as a child?

Here is how my story started: I had just been born. I was in the hospital with my mother. My mother proudly smiled up into my father's face as he walked through the door of her hospital room with my four-year-old brother holding his hand. Bending down, my father picked up my brother, who was trying to peep into my crib. "This is your sister you prayed for," my father said. There was a moment of silence. Then a very disappointed voice said: "Look at her, how red she is, and she can't even play." And with that, my brother wiggled out of my father's arms and walked out of the room!

Four years passed. A child's best teacher when you are four is your brother of eight. I cannot remember a lot about being four, but my brother Jack loves to tell the story of how he used to hide under the bed in his room, waiting for me to look for him. He would wait until he could see my little feet standing in front of the bed. Then he would hit the wooden floor between those two feet with his fist as hard as he could. He had a moment of joy when those feet went up into the air. Next moment, there were tears and screaming, and he had some explaining to do to our mother. At the age of eight, you do not really understand your kind of fun can be a scary experience to someone else. His next move was to wait behind a door until I walked into the room, and then he shouted: "Boo!" The effect was the same. Frightened tears for me and great fun for Jack.

Our parents were too busy to take much notice of our squabbles, and we never stayed angry with each other for long. One day, witnessing my distress, my father put me on his lap and whispered in my ear I should do the same to Jack. That worked! I learned a very good lesson at the age of four. It is powerful to hide behind a door and scare your big brother. This little incident was the first recollection I have of being frightened. It made me very cautious when I was looking for Jack, but with time, I learned he was playing a game of hide and seek when I called him and he did not answer me.

Write Your Story:

- What is your first recollection of fear?
- Write down who was your teacher and at what age you were introduced to fear.

Handling Fear Means Being Brave

"I learned that courage was not the absence of fear, but the triumph over it. The brave man is not he who does not feel afraid, but he who conquers that fear."

— Nelson Mandela

"Be brave now." "Don't be a sissy." "Don't be silly; there is nothing to be afraid of."

Did you hear these or similar words as a child from someone older and wiser than you?

I grew up in a farming community in a semi-desert area of South Africa in the early 1950s, which meant no electricity and no television. Due to the immense heat during the summer months, we slept outside on a veranda or even carried our beds where the cool night air could cool down the lukewarm sheets. Our entertainment in the evenings was watching the stars. The biggest thrill was to find the first satellite going through the night air and watch "the little star" until it was gone. I loved the times of the full moon. Those warm, peaceful evenings when I could see the whole landscape, always held a special magic for me, and I fell asleep feeling safe in my own little world. As farm children, we grew up with knowledge of snakes and scorpions; they were not as scary to me as being sent to fetch something alone in the dark house.

I don't know whether my parents were aware of my fear of the dark and were trying to teach me a lesson or whether they sent me because I was the youngest. I knew it would not help to say I was afraid, and at eight years old, I was trying my best not to let Jack see my fear. The grownups would just say: "Don't be silly; we are right here. There is nothing to be afraid of." Jack would offer to go with me, but if he did, he would scare me even more by making horrible sounds. My solution to this dilemma was to run into and out of that dark house as fast as I could to get back to the safety of my bed outside under the stars. Every time I was back in my bed, I felt proud of myself for "not showing" my fear to the family.

My mom was my best friend, so one day, I confided in her about my fear of the dark. "All my hair on my neck will stand up, my skin feels clammy, and I cannot speak." Mom told me she was also afraid as a child.

The way she had solved the problem was to take a candle and go into the darkest room in their house. She closed the door and first looked at the room in the candlelight. Then she blew out the candle. Her story gave me so much courage. I knew if Mom could face and overcome her fear of the dark, so could I.

Eighteen years later, when I was a young married mother with two little babies asleep in their rooms and my husband was away from home, I had to deal with that fear again. Only then did I realise it was not the dark I feared, but what could be lurking in the dark. We were living in a big city that was not as safe as the area where I grew up. I would walk from window to window, scaring myself with all kinds of thoughts and wondering if I had to choose, which child I would take to flee with. Then one night, I remembered my mother's words, so I walked out into the dark garden to stand there until I felt safe and calm. I realised in that moment my fear of what might be hiding in the darkness was only thoughts in my mind. I walked back into the house with the same feeling of pride and joy I had felt as an eight-year old child when I triumphed over my fear of going into a dark house. With a prayer of thanks on my lips, I got into bed, knowing I had released my fear of the dark forever.

If you bring light into the darkness by facing your fear, you see that darkness is nothing more than not having a light, and fear is nothing more than a thought in your mind. There is a saying: Fear stands for False Evidence Appearing Real.

Write Your Story:

- What scared you as a child about the dark, or what was hiding in your mind about what the darkness could bring?
- In your notes write what you can do to light up your darkness and expel a fear you have.

Being Alone Or Bored Can Be Good For You

"Loneliness expresses the pain of being alone
and solitude expresses the glory of being alone."
— Paul Tillich

Do you know what it feels like to be lonely or bored? Have you felt that slight feeling of panic when you have nothing to do or when no one has time for you? It is almost as if you are not seen.

The year I started high school, Jack left home for his year in military service. I missed Jack very much and wrote him long letters. High school was a scary place for me. With Jack being away from home, our parents became even more protective of me. Going to a new school much bigger than the previous one and not knowing anybody was difficult for me. I was unsure of myself and very shy. To crown it all, my best friend of seven years made new friends, while I found myself struggling to make friends and to get accepted into the groups. I had an overwhelming feeling of loneliness amidst all those children. Sometimes I looked and listened to the voices and laughter around me and thought I had nothing in common with anybody. By then, I knew you do not show your fear or talk about it, and I just quietly joined the groups of girls where I could be unnoticed and unseen during breaks.

My parents saw me change from an outgoing, confident child who did well in sport and on an academic level to a quiet, shy girl. The highlight of my day was in the afternoons after school or during holidays. There were many big trees on the farm, and I would climb into the big mulberry tree near the house. There, between the thick green leaves, I could lie on my back on the branches, stare at the blue sky through the leaves, and let my thoughts take flight. There was also a Syringa tree in the back of the house. I spent lots of time taking Jack's pellet gun up into that tree to practice target shooting by looking over my shoulder in a mirror. My parents made a big fuss about my ability to shoot by aiming in the mirror, so I slowly started to get my confidence back. I still admire their courage in allowing me to do something as potentially dangerous as climbing into a tree with a pellet gun, but it showed me they trusted me and had confidence in me. So many things could have gone wrong! I studied very hard, and by the end of my third year in high school, I was one of the school's top students. Although I regained some of my old spark, I always felt as if I were not really one of the popular girls. I withdrew into myself and was marked by the other children as "stuck-up." I still escaped into the trees to get away from people. My best friend in those lonely, difficult years was my mom, and I sometimes missed her terribly when I was at school. Jack was away at university and had a steady girlfriend, which further added to me feeling alone.

Now many years later, I listen with a smile as my grandchildren complain that they are bored when they cannot play games on their tablets or watch videos on television. How times have changed. Society today is all about the busyness of life, and with the overload of social media, people try to relax by listening to music or talks while walking the dog, not realising that it is more of the same. Living in New Zealand, I am always amazed when I go for a walk in the beautiful parks or on the beach and see people with earphones on, oblivious to the sounds and beauty around them.

It took me many years to understand my withdrawal into my beloved trees when I felt lonely was a form of meditation and good for me. The Buddha said anxiety, fears, and suffering come from minds overpowered by delusion and distraction. Our minds are like a "drunk monkey in a thorn tree", wild and untamed, but what if we can tame the mind? Then nothing can frighten us because all fear comes from a mind that is untamed.

Unless we sit quietly with no distractions or outside entertainment, we will always react to life as perceived by the mind. In hindsight, I realised I learned so much about myself in those quiet, alone times in the trees. I never felt lonely up in those trees. While I was sitting or lying in the arms of my beloved trees, the wind swaying those big branches as they softly cradled me into inner peacefulness, one thing was sure — I never felt bored. In fact, I started to like being alone on the farm with nobody really paying attention to me. It was in those moments that I could go into the safe, green haven between the leaves and just be me. I learned in those years that I never felt more alone than being among noisy teenagers who were all trying in their own way to fit in while forming their own set of rules for life.

Write Your Story:

- Did you also experience feeling left out or alone as a teenager?
- Write down what you did or are doing to find inner peace and quiet.

Getting A "First Cut"

"Your children are the greatest gift God will give to you and their souls the heaviest responsibility He will place in your hands. Take time with them; teach them to have faith in God. Be a person in whom they can have faith. When you are old, nothing else you've done will have mattered as much."

— Lisa Wingate

The "first cut" is the first time when something happens to you as a child and the reaction of the people closest to you. That imprint stays with you all your life, causing you to react according to that imprint.

Did you feel safe and protected by your parents?

I grew up in a Christian home and still remember my dad reading from the Bible every evening after supper. Then we would pray and sing a hymn. I was not so fond of the prayer part because we had to kneel and I got tired, but my mom had a lovely voice, and I loved the singing. The feeling of safety and seeing my parents humbly kneeling at their chairs every evening stayed with me all my life. As a child, I believed God and my parents loved us and would protect us from any harm.

I have often said I am glad I grew up before everything was labelled. When I was about six or seven, our neighbours were an elderly couple. They were good and kind people. My mom would send me at least twice a week to take them milk or eggs. Sometimes Mom or Jack would go with me, but many times I had to go on my own.

I liked walking to the neighbours' house until one day when I saw the old man standing behind the bushes close to the path where I had to walk. I found it strange that he called out quietly to me, but I walked over to him. To my horror, he bent down and kissed me on my mouth. I turned around and ran home, knowing instinctively I did not like what had just happened.

I ran into the kitchen and blurted out the whole incident to my mom. When she heard he was waiting for me on the side of the road, she looked a little disturbed. Then she said in a calm voice: "Next time you pretend not to hear him, and if you see him hiding next to the road, turn around and come back."

That was exactly what I did because even in my innocence, I knew something was not right. It was only years later I heard the words paedophile and sexual abuse. I often wonder whether my fear and scarring would have been more permanent and deeper if my mother had reacted with disgust and made a big scene. I just thought he was a silly old man, and I could outrun him any time.

This incident was another piece of my domestication into a fear-filled world. It was a "first cut" about trust, as I lost some of my innocent trust in all people that day. I always made sure the old man never got me alone again. Many years later, in my own colour healing and life coaching practice, I cried when a client left. During the session, she told me she was sexually abused by her grandfather. Where do you run to when your mother does not believe you, and how hard must it be to trust again if someone so close to you is the offender? My experience with the old neighbour was my first lesson about trust. And it happened long before I would learn trust is in me. Living with fear and being scared makes it impossible to trust. Living with love and seeing everything as sacred makes trust blossom like the wildflowers after the rain.

Write Your Story:
- What happened to you to break the trusting innocence you had as a child?
- Write the biggest issue or the name of the person who caused you to lose your trust in people as a child.

Summary
We are born without fear and then we get "domesticated." A child's best teacher is often just a little bit older. It is a powerful feeling to hide behind a door and scare your big brother when you are four years old. The best way of dealing with fear is to do that which we fear. Fear is in your mind, and you experience a feeling of triumph and joy when you break free of it.

High school can be a scary place. You can feel lonely in the midst of many people.

It is almost a lifestyle in today's society always to be busy. Our minds are like a "drunk monkey in a thorn tree", wild and untamed. With such minds, we react to life as we perceive it, which is not necessarily the truth. Taming our minds will stop the fear.

The "first cut" is the first time when something happens to you as a child and the reaction of the people closest to you. That imprint stays with you all your life, causing you to react according to the emotions around the first cut.

The Biggest Lessons

We are born without fear, but through the process of reward and punishment, we are motivated through fear. We learn to do according to what we are told or else we have to suffer the consequences. There are only two ways to get attention — by being good or being bad.

Word Reveal And The Power Of Words

In the word *Scared* is *Sacred* and also cared, dare, red, read, and dear. We can either go through life scared of everything we may do wrong, or rather, not do right, or we can see everything as a lesson and as sacred and honour ourselves through the learning experience. The choice is ours.

Rainbow Blessing

Thank you for loving parents and grandparents who protect their children.

We bless children everywhere who are scared and alone, and we surround them with Pink and Blue Rays for Love and Protection.

"Neither a man nor a crowd nor a nation
can be trusted to act humanely or to think sanely
under the influence of a great fear."
— Bertrand Russell

Chapter 2 — Freezing With Fright

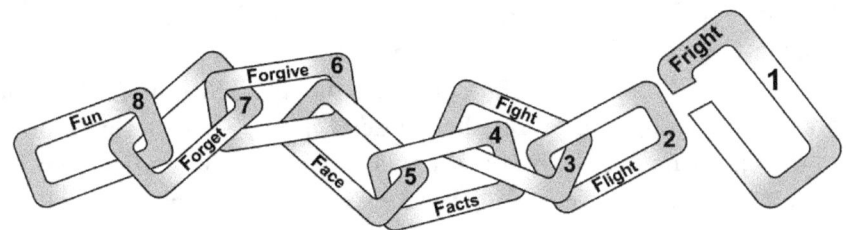

"Your opinion is your opinion; your perception is your perception. Do not confuse them with facts or truth."
— John Moore

In the previous chapter, we discussed how we are born without fear and then get "domesticated." As children, we learn to "handle" our fear in various ways. The way we handle fear is often influenced by the "first cut" — the first time we get hurt or get sick and how the people around us react to our pain. In this chapter, we will see how the fear-filled world teaches us to live with fear and that our perceptions — which are not necessarily true — rule our world. Using the Fright-Flight-Fight reaction to fear, we look at *Frighters* in this chapter.

Frightening Experiences Can "Freeze" You Up for a Lifetime

Have you ever had such a fright you could not move or speak?

I never had a problem with speaking. My mom loved to tell the story about the first morning she took me to school. All the parents were invited for tea in the staff room, and when they left after about half an hour, my mom heard the teacher say: "Jansie, please turn around and stop talking."

It was only a few months later something happened to give me such a fright that I was literally speechless for a while. Growing up in a farming community and attending a little farm school had its privileges. About a kilometre from the school was a small general dealer. It was a highlight of the day if the teacher trusted you enough to send you to the shop during school time to "quickly" get something she needed. My best friend, Betty, and I were sent to the shop one morning. Holding hands and chatting all the way, we happily walked there.

As we neared the shop, we saw a big dog sleeping on the step in front. We instantly slowed down, and I could sense the fear creeping into my legs, making them feel weak. As Betty passed the dog, it jumped up and bit her in the back of her thigh. She was in tears. The lady in the shop ran out, and suddenly, amidst the pandemonium, we were surrounded by loving, caring people. Betty was crying so it was left to me to explain what had happened. But to my horror, when the grownups asked me what had happened, I could not utter a single word. At last, as the words came out, I stammered and was so embarrassed that I also started to cry. After we each had a glass of water with sugar for the shock and Betty's leg was inspected — the bite had not broken the skin — we were on our way back to school with the teacher's little parcel in a bag. It took me up to thirty years to overcome my fear of big dogs.

I learned another lesson about fear that day. Shock can freeze you up, and the memory of the shock gets stuck in your body and mind to surface every time you get into a situation that triggers that fear, or until you are willing to heal and let go of the trauma. As we do with our fears, I did not think about how my fear had affected me; I just knew I was afraid of big dogs and avoided them.

I also started to tell myself I did not like to speak in front of people, so I came up with a brilliant excuse. One of my favourite sayings for years was people want to talk and be heard, so I will be the listener. It took me many years to heal that seven-year-old girl's fear of speaking in public — a fear based on feeling embarrassed because I could not give an account of a traumatic incident moments after it happened. Every time I had to speak in public, I projected the feeling of utter panic onto the situation.

Write Your Story:

- What happened in your life that frightened you so much you froze and could not speak or act in that moment?
- Have you healed the fear, or are you making excuses to avoid working with it?
- Write about one incident where you could not move or speak.

- Then write about how you overcame the problem or how you intend to overcome the fear.

Suppressing Versus Expressing Our Feelings

Do you find you suppress words you want to express just to keep the peace? Do you express yourself and then feel guilty or think you said it all in the wrong words?

One of my favourite sayings is "By the time we can talk about the hurt, we have already worked a lot on the emotional pain."

"You are too sensitive, my love." My mother used these words many times. I was sick a lot as a child. My mother suffered from asthma and hay fever when she was young and I had the same problems as a child.

It was only years later I learned these symptoms manifest in your body when you feel overprotected, stifled, and irritated on an emotional level. The local doctor was a man I did not like at all. I always felt he did not see me as a person. He would walk into the room, tell me to breathe in deeply, put his cold stethoscope on my chest and back, and then, without another word, prescribe medicine. The medicine helped my asthma, but it upset my stomach, causing vomiting and leaving me feeling sicker than the asthma ever did. When my mom enquired about this, the doctor just said it was a "persistent germ" in my tummy, which contributed to me feeling as if I had the plague.

One day when the doctor was on holiday, the locum told my mom I had an allergic reaction to the asthma medication. He prescribed a different medicine. The problem was solved on a physical level, but the experience caused me to distrust doctors and started me on the path to self-healing and homeopathic practices.

I outgrew my asthma, but the hay fever, especially at harvest time, became worse. My mom suggested I go away to another part of the country for the last two years of school. I agreed with Mom and was very excited because I had several good reasons to take this step. Firstly, the school was much closer to Jack, who was only fifteen minutes away at university. Secondly, it was one of the best schools in the country. Thirdly, I did not really have close friends at school, so my teenage mind thought it would be great to get away from home.

Write Your Story:

- Name one event in your school life that frightened you so much you suppressed your feelings and could not speak about it.
- In your own document, write down whether you were the kind of person who suppressed your feelings or expressed them.

Learning Appreciation And Eating Disorders

Do you eat when you are bored or get stressed, or do you stop eating when life gets stressful?

Saying goodbye to my dad and seeing him cry for the first time in my life, I realised leaving home could be a bigger step than I had anticipated. I had to share a room with three other girls and adapt to new rules. I quickly became best friends, in fact lifelong friends, with two of the girls in my room. Unfortunately, my new friends did not keep me from falling back into my "withdrawal pattern" as I usually did when I got scared or unsure of myself. Studying for long hours was my way of proving I could make it and that I was a fighter.

The first six months at the new school, due to my emotionally "frozen" state, I spoke very little, except when spoken to. Elmarie, my best friend, was an outgoing, very popular, friendly girl, and she did a lot to get me out of my dark moments. I learned a valuable life lesson in those first six months — you sometimes only value something or someone once you have lost it.

Being far away from my parents for the first time made me realise how much I loved them and how great they were. The shock of being separated from my beloved parents, always being surrounded by other people, and listening to the unhappy stories of some of the girls in the dorm, opened my eyes to how lucky I was to grow up in such a happy and caring family — and also to have the freedom of growing up on a farm. The main reason I did not speak was because I was afraid if I said something, I might start to cry. Suppressing my longing for my parents and my home, I studied more and more. The rule was everybody studied together in a big hall, but I soon got my own little "study room" where I could carry on for hours after normal study time. I have always been grateful to my dorm parents, who were clever and compassionate enough to see how much I needed my own quiet space.

In those days, I measured my self-worth by my academic achievements. All the studying paid off in the form of academic achievements, but it did not do much for my popularity. To fill up the emptiness and pain on the inside, I started to eat more. I did not know about eating disorders in 1969. All I knew was I was constantly missing my parents, my home, and my room — in short, all the familiar things I had grown up with. I did not give too much attention to it, although I gained twelve kilograms. Going home on my first holiday, my mom could not hide her concern that I had put on so much weight.

A very unhealthy pattern of overeating and dieting developed. At one stage, I started a diet on a Monday of having only a cup of black coffee for breakfast and a hardboiled egg in the evening. On Thursday, I fainted, and the matron brought me toast with tea. Today, I can still recall how I could literally feel life coming back into me with every mouthful of food I chewed! I learned two good lessons from this experience: No diet really works unless you change your thinking pattern, and food has got everything to do with our emotional wellbeing.

The good part of me being away from home was that I had three friends sharing a room with me. I also became very independent and valued my family much more.

In our last year of school, my two friends and I were elected by the children and teachers as leaders. I saw this as another achievement to make my parents proud and another responsibility on top of my studies. I did the job diligently, but I felt stifled and not able to express how I really felt. To everybody's surprise, I did not want to go to university; instead, I opted for a year in college where I could do a secretarial course.

My parents went along with my decision. Years later, I discovered they were afraid I would push myself too much to achieve high scores at university. I realised I must have been a real pain for many people while in school. I was a total perfectionist and took life far too seriously for a seventeen-year-old teenager.

Write Your Story:

Reacting to everyday stress, we either eat the wrong food, overindulge, or stop eating altogether. Acknowledging where you are and getting help is the first step to breaking the emotional pattern.

- Do you know the emotional trigger that causes your eating disorder?
- Make notes how you want to solve your problem.

Searching For Happiness Outside Ourselves

Have you ever thought your life would be perfect if you could get a boyfriend or girlfriend, or if you had money?

My friend Peter always said poor people are better off than rich people because poor people still think if you have money, life will be without problems. I think it is the same with love. When we are lonely, we think someone else can take the loneliness away and make us happy.

My college year in Cape Town was one of the most carefree years of my life. After two years in boarding school, I was used to being away from home, which made it much easier to adapt to college life. Being a leader for most of my time in school and knowing how difficult it can be always to set a good example, I truly appreciated the leaders in the college dorm.

I also enjoyed the freedom of being an ordinary student. I felt alive for the first time, allowing myself to enjoy college life and not study all the time.

A few good things happened during my college year. I met my future husband and, without any effort, started to lose some of the weight I had picked up in high school. The happy, trusting, outgoing four-year-old child had now grown into a radiantly happy young woman in her nineteenth year.

I started working the next year and had a wonderful time in my first job as a secretary for a general manager of a big company. I became good friends with the managing director's secretary, who was a few years older than me and she taught me more about the work than my studies had. I worked for eight months and then moved to another city to be closer to my fiancé. I got a job working for the senior partner in a law firm and enjoyed every moment of it, but I started to realise I did not want to be in an administrative job all my life, especially in a law firm.

Weldon and I got married when I was twenty, and soon afterwards, I became pregnant with our first child. It was the first grandchild on both sides of the family, and everybody was very excited — except me.

I suffered from persistent morning sickness at all hours of the day and, therefore, I did not enjoy a big part of my pregnancy.

Being young, happy, and healthy, the downside of my pregnancy was forgotten the moment Brian was born. I stepped into the role of full-time mother with ease and joy. Three years later, our daughter, Anri, was born. My second pregnancy had more complications, and I lost so much weight my family worried I was anorexic. I remember thinking, *A few years back they worried about me being overweight; now they worry about me being underweight!*

I loved being a full-time mom, and my whole life was focused on my husband, our two children, and making a home for them. For a while, life was good.

Write Your Story:

• What have you done that made you happy?
• Make a note if you experienced a big event that really made you feel alive and fulfilled.

Falling Into the Pit of Depression

"I don't think people understand how stressful it is to explain what's going on in your head when you don't even understand it yourself."

— Sara Quin

Have you ever felt anxious, stressed, or depressed?

At the age of twenty-five, I had a normal life like many other young, married people of my generation. Weldon was working very hard to build his career. I never had a problem with being on my own, but being alone with the children all day, while my husband worked long hours, caused me to feel frustrated and worthless. I fell back into my old habits and worked harder in my home and garden to "fight" the feelings of inferiority and hopelessness.

I have always been amazed when people behave normally and then you hear they have taken their own lives or had a nervous breakdown. Without me noticing it, my thoughts became more and more dark and without hope. One evening when my husband was working late, I took his revolver out of the cupboard and sat with it in my lap, thinking I was a good shot and it would be over in seconds. At that moment, I heard my young son coming down the passage. In a split second, I realised I could not do it to my two young children — I could not shoot myself while they were alone with me. I put the gun away, but a gripping fear took hold of me — a feeling that I had fallen into a pit of darkness.

I wanted to save my family from living and dealing with the stigma that surrounded depression in those days. I was seen as a fighter in my family and giving up or falling apart was not an option. I decided I would deal with the depression on my own. I had no idea how to fight the sickness; in fact, I did not even think it was a sickness. I just knew I was feeling so alone and godforsaken. I felt cut off from God, and although I still went to church with my family, I felt no connection to the Divine.

I felt God did not hear my prayers and the church was of no help in strengthening my trust in the Divine. In fact, I started to see all the shortcomings in religion and became disillusioned with the church, feeling angry and ashamed, and blaming God and religion for my unhappiness. I rebelled against religion, and in my moments of utter despair, I told Jesus I would not follow Him anymore. I felt if He was real, He could find me!

Since then, I have studied many of the world's principal religions. I came to the conclusion that the core belief in all religions has truth — namely, there is a loving presence known as God. God has many names and all religions believe God is love, forgiveness, and all the good we are trying so hard to follow.

I believe we are a Spirit living in an earthly body as our vehicle. Since we have chosen a body as our structure, it makes sense to me that a part of our earthly lessons will be to learn about structure. Churches and religions give us structure for our spiritual lives. In spite of the shortcomings in religions, I am glad I experienced faith and religion as a child.

Understandably, people are resisting religion all over the world because of the horrific abuse of power in the name of religion, and it is good those atrocities are in the open. Although many religions preach about the love, forgiveness, and peace of a God-centred life, people have been tortured and killed and many wars have been fought under that pretence. Many religions and religious leaders still hold on to their power with fear motivation and keep their followers from experiencing universal love. What was clear to me in those dark and early days of my journey was I could not turn to religion for help with my depression.

Although I tried to keep my depressive state from my family, my mom, being emotionally close to me, sensed something was wrong and tried through telephone calls and her supportive letters to help me deal with my depression. Nobody in my family had any experience of depression, so I soon realised I would have to help myself.

Maybe I was ashamed of being seen as weak. With a deep sense of wisdom, I knew I had to work with this lesson in my own way. It became a journey in which I often felt total despair that I would not be able to heal myself. During the darkest moments, I always found an inner strength to get up and carry on. The mornings when my family left for school and work were the hardest. I had no strength to do anything. Guilt was my biggest problem. I felt guilty about letting everybody down and not being able to snap out of my feelings of utter desolation.

Write Your Story:

- Have you suffered from anxiety or depression?
- Write a few sentences about your feelings when you were or are depressed.

Climbing Out of the Pit

> *"When you have depression,*
> *simply existing is a full-time job."*
> — Author Unknown

Have you felt totally alone and godforsaken in your life? In one of my old diaries, I wrote:

I am in a dark pit sitting in the corner. There is nothing in this pit except me and despair. How do I get out of this pit? I feel totally numb. Knowing about the fright-flight-fight phenomena and that, depending on the situation, you react accordingly, I admit to myself in this pit of darkness I am definitely in fright reaction — in fact, I am totally frozen. On the outside, I must look normal as people treat me like normal, but on the inside, I am frozen like an ice statue. I do not even know how it happened, why I feel like this. How will I get out of this pit of depression? The next day, I wrote in my diary:

One moment at a time. It is too hard for me to try to get out of the pit, but if I can have one moment a day of joy, of not feeling there is no hope, then tomorrow I can have two moments of joy, and for the rest of the day, I can sit in my pit and, as my friend Douwe used to say: "Go deeper into the depression and enjoy being depressed!"

After long weeks of working every day to have more and more joyful moments, one morning I realised I had enough moments of joy to say I was out of the pit. The next note in my diary read:

I thought everybody who loves me would be glad I am not so depressed anymore, but nobody was waiting with bated breath on the outside of the pit! Note to Me: Depression is your lesson; everybody else is busy with their own lives.

I slipped back down that pit many times, but never again to the bottom.

I kept myself out of the pit with "*one moment of joy at a time.*"

When I tell people about getting out of the pit, I warn them just when you reach the top of your pit, someone may step on your hands by saying or doing something that can send you back down. Do not take it personally. That person is also busy living his or her life and probably not aware of your depression. This understanding will also make you stronger and more courageous.

I read widely about depression and addictions. I realised people can become addicted to anything, and depression is like an addiction, or may be part of or due to an addiction. The problem is that the world still has acceptable addictions and unacceptable addictions. I tested this theory by telling people, "I am a workaholic." Mostly, the reaction was, "Be glad you don't smoke, drink, or do drugs." An addiction, no matter what it is, always has devastating effects on the person and his or her close family. I wrote in my diary:

I admit due to many factors in my life, I am a workaholic. I value myself through the work I do, and I feel worthless being a mom and a housewife because I do not earn any money. My depression is the result of years of suppressing myself and trying to please others. I have become a poisonous pleaser.

In hindsight, I acknowledged I studied far more than was necessary in school, and then I carried the "good" habit into my marriage. It is also very easy to replace one addiction with another since people who stop smoking or drinking alcohol can get addicted to chocolates or food. Just like alcoholics who cannot say after years of being sober, they can go to the pub and not drink, people with depression have to accept they can fall back into their patterns of behaviour if the "right" buttons are pushed. It was difficult for me to find the balance as a workaholic. It is not an addiction that you can totally walk away from or avoid.

In my mind, I made up a lovely little story about my pit, getting out of it, and then realising there was no welcoming committee of family and friends to congratulate me for defeating depression. I had the choice of feeling sorry for myself or starting to walk away from the pit. I learned we cannot run away from fear. At that stage of my journey, I was still finding answers and acknowledged to myself that my reaction in this particular situation was to freeze out of fear, with almost devastating results. It was by far one of my biggest lessons I had to overcome in my life.

Write Your Story:

- What do you do when you are afraid, anxious, or depressed?
- Write your notes how you feel when you are in your pit of depression.

Travelling The Desert Road

> *"It's your road and yours alone.*
> *Others may walk it with you,*
> *but no one can walk it for you."*
>
> — Rumi

Have you felt in your life that strangers understand you better than your close family?

I call this part of my journey the *desert road*, but most people talk about the dark night of the soul. It was during this time I understood with great wisdom that every person is the only one in his or her own universe. That discovery made it easier for me to walk my *desert road* because I knew no one in my family could help me, and I could not expect them to understand — they were not walking in my shoes and it was my lesson. My mantra changed from *one moment at a time* to *one step at a time*.

The saying "like attracts like" soon became a reality on my journey. I met with fellow *desert travellers*. They were also depressed or in various stages of working through depression. It was interesting for me to realise that they were from all levels of society, and many were highly educated, brilliant, rich, and very wise. In the days of sitting in my pit, I had formed a lot of perceptions about why I had depression. I concluded that I was not worth much — I had no degree and made no money as a stay-at-home mom. Once I had that perception fixed in my mind, I found evidence supporting it everywhere.

Meeting people on the desert road who had degrees, power, and money helped me see the truth in the Dalai Lama's words:

> If a person's basic state of mind is serene and calm, then it is possible for this inner peace to overwhelm a painful physical experience. On the other hand, if someone is suffering from depression, anxiety, or any form of emotional distress, then even if he or she happens to be enjoying physical comforts, he or she will not really be able to experience the happiness that these could bring.

Travelling the *desert road*, I found many new friends who accepted me without any expectations.

Write Your Story:

- Can you name a situation in your life where you felt you had more support from strangers than close family?
- Write a few sentences about your *desert road* and how much you have grown during a lonely and difficult time.

Finding The Oasis

"Your big opportunity may be right where you are now."
— Napoleon Hill

Are you searching for answers that will help you on your self-healing journey?

Rediscovering the beauty within ourselves is like the Buddha said: "No one saves us but ourselves. No one can and no one may. We ourselves must walk the path." In the process of finding ME (My Energy), which meant working with my energy and learning how to manage many of my fears, I referred to myself as *living in the desert*. I met many other *desert dwellers* who were on their journeys of self-discovery. Some of the paths I followed were good, others only mirages. I realised many people I met were also hurting and seeking, and they made me more aware of my own shortcomings. In the end, they were as valuable as the good teachers I had.

I had a saying in those days: I have learned more from dishonest people in six months than from honest people in twenty years. I did many courses with great teachers and read many books by wonderful, inspiring authors, but the oasis in the desert came to me when I was introduced to the Investment in Excellence programme from the Pacific Institute® (TPI). This particular programme opened a whole new world for me. The institute's website sums it up wonderfully:

> The Pacific Institute (TPI) believes that people are the cornerstone of organisational success, and Investment in Excellence® develops this most valuable asset. It is a powerful development experience that enables individuals and organisations to achieve much more of their potential by changing their perception of what is possible, and then providing the skills, knowledge, and application to cause a change in what they actually accomplish.

My husband and I were both trained as facilitators for this programme, and we also introduced our children, who were young teenagers at that stage, to the programme. I started implementing the process in my own life. I realised my perceptions about myself were not the truth, and that perceptions can be so powerful that they can bankrupt a company if enough people start to "lock-on" to the same perceptions.

My self-confidence improved rapidly as I studied and read up on self-improvement. What surprised me was although many organisations bought the programme and provided training to employees, unless employees felt the programme could help on a personal level, for them it was just another training course. It was also very important to get the right people to drive the programme in the organisations. My conclusion was that during the "domestication" process, we all become "unconscious," and many of us go through a lifetime without "waking" up to our true potential. I love the anonymous quote: "Just because you're breathing doesn't mean you're alive."

Write Your Story:

- Have you found the *wow* moment in the search for your truth?
- Write a short paragraph about how it happened for you.
- If you are still looking for that special key to your heart, read on— maybe you will find an answer in this book.

Trumping With The Wild Card

(A wild card has particular power to help you.)

Were you one of the many people frightened because Donald Trump won the 2016 presidential election in the United States of America?

We only have to watch or read the news of the day to hear about the disastrous decisions politicians make on a daily basis. I have never heard anybody ask themselves, "Why is that person irritating me so much, or why am I reacting with so much fear to this situation? Can it be that there is a part of me that is like that political leader?" I started asking these questions after I was trained as a facilitator for Investment in Excellence. Seeing high profile people in the world as our teachers who challenge us through their words and behaviour to look at ourselves, instead of buying into the fear motivation from various news sources, may be a powerful wild card to wake you up.

I wrote this to a wonderful "wild card" in my life: The anger in both of us had to be tamed to become a beautiful flowing stream of energy. The dark clouds of Violet and indigo when faced bravely — changed into soft rays of spiritual oneness — magical moments! We filled our yellow raw fear with laughter. The trust we thought we lacked were built through the joys we shared when we walked into the soft green woods of our hearts, telling our true stories. Now we can dance together in spirit — two people seemingly very different yet so alike wanting the same things in life. Instead of freezing with fear, we feel joy and gratitude — unfolding like a beautiful sunrise with vibrant orange colours — the promise of a new beginning.

Summary

Our perceptions, which are not necessarily true, rule our world. Shock can *freeze* our feelings, and it can take years for those frozen feelings to heal. Reacting to fear as a *Frighter*, we may seem normal to the outside world, but suppressing our feelings can lead to eating disorders or addictions.

We should not depend on others to make us happy. Shame, blame, and guilt are fear-based feelings that cause many people to suffer anxiety or depression.

Live life *one moment at a time*, and make that moment a joyful one. We cannot run away from fear. Do not blame other people for your addictions or depression, but see them as your lessons or initiations to find your truth. Find your answers on the *desert road* we all have to walk at some point. It is on the *desert road* you will find the oasis that will open your heart to live your life to its fullest. If life gets too hard, take it *one step at a time.*

The Biggest Lessons

Some people will freeze when they get scared. They find it difficult to talk about what is happening to them. In my Rainbow World, I call them the *Frighters*. Taking responsibility for our lessons in life is the first step to recovery.

Word Reveal And The Power Of Words

In the word *Frighters*, the fear words are grief, regret, hit, and Fighters, to name a few. *Frighters* often feel *overwhelmed*, blaming others because they feel shame and guilt themselves for freezing in fear situations.

Rainbow Blessing

May the frightened people all over the world be enfolded in soft gold and turquoise rays to give them courage to speak up and overcome their addictions.

Chapter 3 — Taking Flight

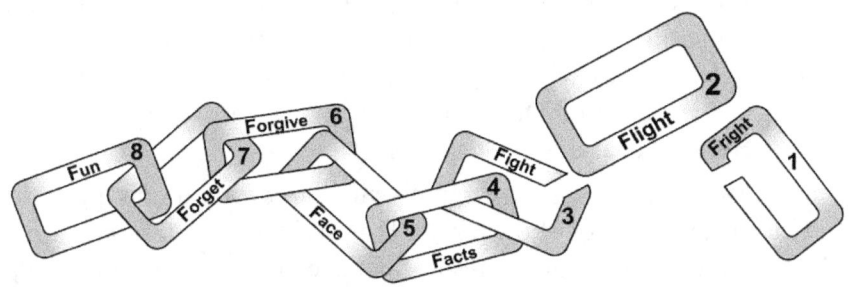

*"Peace is not the absence of conflict;
it is the ability to handle conflict by peaceful means."*
— Ronald Reagan

In Chapter 2, I discussed the "Frighters." They are frozen with fear and often too numb to take any action. In this chapter, we look at the "Flighters", the quiet ones who try to keep the peace at all costs.

Riding On The *Fear Bus*

*"If you avoid conflict to keep the peace,
you start a war inside yourself."*
— Cheryl Richardson

Do you avoid conflict at all costs?

After my ordeal with depression and walking into the desert, I called myself a *desert dweller*. Although I was sitting in the middle of my new life, I still wanted to stay in the safety of the desert I had created in my mind, for a while longer.

My journey made me very aware of how I react when confronted with fear-filled situations. My desert was full of fear-filled people. If we are living with fear, 80 percent of our thoughts are repetitive or negative. We act the way we think, and therefore, the devastating effects fear has in our world are no surprise. All my courses are based on changing behaviour patterns from fear to love. Humour is one technique I use in my classes to help people change. During my *desert years*, I started talking about the *fear and love bus* because I realised I could fill a few buses with people who are travelling the same journey of unlearning about fear in order to live love. I often use the powerful and very personal language of colour to help people heal themselves through their colour choices of the Coloured Oils and Sprays I work with. (More about my Colour Healing Therapy in Chapter 19.)

My husband is an absolute genius when it comes to making slides, and he created the slide show for my *Fear and Love Motivation* courses, which I call ME. The courses are all about becoming aware of our energy (our thoughts, feelings, words, and actions) and changing it from fear-based to love-based. In changing, we find the real *ME* (my energy). My husband and I had to learn to work together as a team on this project, and I can honestly say the fear bus sometimes went "off road." But in the end, I had my wonderful presentation.

At tea break during one of my *ME* courses, a delegate said the following: "I like this *fear bus*. I am the driver of that bus. I am a very angry person because of fear, and my wife and children have had a hard time living with me. Tonight, I am going to tell my family about fear and the *fear bus*. Being aware of my fear, I am going to change, and from now on, my family and I are going to learn how to manage our fears on this bus."

We cannot run away from fear. Fear lives in our minds and our bodies react to that fear. We live in a world of duality. We have to learn about fear in order to start to find the love in ourselves. Accepting I am on the *fear bus* with many other people made it easier for me to concentrate on being mindful of every moment. Shame, blame, and guilt are the luggage we bring with us on the *fear bus*.

Write Your Story:

- By reading this book, you have already joined me on the fear bus.
- Write down what "luggage" you are bringing.
- Are you blaming others for your life circumstances, or do you live in shame and guilt about situations that happened to you?

Finding Book Teachers And Putting It In The Pot

"When the student is ready, the teacher will appear."
— Buddha

My teachers came to me in the form of books. I am a firm believer books can bring you the whole world. I have read all of Linda Goodman's books, and her *Star Signs* is still one of my favourites.

As a child in fourth grade, I loved it when the teacher gave us a word and we had to see how many other words we could make out of it. In Linda Goodman's *Star Signs*, I learned about "word druids", and my love for and ability to see words within a word became one of my favourite hobbies. Reading *The Four Agreements* by Don Miguel Ruiz, who speaks about being "impeccable with your word", helped me to understand the deeper meaning of words, and again, my love and respect for words was taken to a higher level.

All through my struggle with depression, I tried to be a dedicated mother and wife, but my safety blanket was to go into the *desert* in my mind. I was building a whole new life for myself — helping other people, and in the process, becoming whole again. I was growing rapidly at a level of which my family was not always aware. After years of working on myself, I did not expect people to understand what I had worked through and how much it took to come out of the darkness of depression into the place of light I was creating in my own mind.

My husband and children were all successful in their own ways, but I still worked on myself and my feelings of inferiority. The Investment in Excellence programme was the key opening many doors for me. In my effort to find my own answers, I became a "course junky", attending self-development courses and learning from highly spiritual people.

I always had a good relationship with my children and shared my new philosophies with them. My teenage son started to bring friends home who were "depro" (a word they used for feeling down or depressed) — this normally happened after a breakup with a girl or a fall out with a parent. I introduced a "POT" system to the kids. I had a big, three-legged iron pot with a lid. South Africans love making food in these pots, so I knew everybody would associate the pot with food and good times. I told the kids the pot was symbolic of the place where we put our problems or questions. We were both contributing to the "stew" in the pot.

I explained to them the only rule was they could not do anything drastic unless they had been back to the pot. I told them I was legally obliged to tell their parents, a teacher, social worker, or psychologist if they were really depressed and planning dangerous actions. But if they abided by the one rule to first come back to the pot, they would be okay. Most of them just wanted to be heard. They didn't really need advice. They needed someone to listen to them. Putting their sorrows in the pot gave them the distance to see the situation in perspective, and normally when they came back after one week, they were confident enough and ready to burn the "stuff" in the pot. I often encourage people to talk to someone they can trust or put their problems in the pot. Either way, you need to get suppressed feelings out of your system before you become physically sick.

Write Your Story:
- What would you like to put in the pot?
- Maybe you have a problem or a secret you have been carrying around for a long time without sharing it with anyone.
- Write down what you would like to put into your pot.

Devastating Natural Disasters Cause Confusing Reactions

"The quality of our lives depends not on whether or not we have conflicts, but on how we respond to them."
— Tom Crum

Have you ever been part of a natural disaster like a flood, earthquake, hurricane, tornado, or tsunami?

Growing up on the banks of the Orange River in South Africa, I saw what floods can do and how powerless we are when it comes to nature. It was difficult for me to fathom the magnitude and power of that river as a child. In the dry season, it could be a small stream we could swim in or even walk through at certain places. Then in the rainy season, it could rise and overflow its banks, taking everything in its path. My father used to say you could feel the water's pulsating energy when it was coming down in a flood.

I always admired the farmers for their acceptance and courage after working for days and nights to try to keep the water away from crops. To stop the flood waters, the farmers made high sand walls along the riverbanks; some walls were higher than houses and so wide tractors could easily ride on top of them.

It is a devastating feeling of loss and hopelessness to watch the water engulfing everything in its wake and to know there will be no crops for a year or more — not to speak of all the work, time, and money to get the land back to its original state. It has been fifty years since I experienced a flood, but I still remember the stench of the mud after the water subsided. Like many others, I looked at the pictures of the devastating tsunami that shocked the world and took the lives of thousands of people on December 26, 2004. People were running away laughing or smiling with this wall of water towering behind them; some were even standing on car roofs taking photos as the water approached. From the photos, I could see those people were in the worst situation imaginable, but it seemed they did not grasp it might be their last smile. I asked myself if that was what happens when we are in *flight reaction to fear*. Do we run away from danger while smiling, not realising death is right behind us? Talking to my friend Tiriana after the Kaikoura earthquake in New Zealand, she said, "They kept warning people about the tsunami that could follow. Considering the energy of the quake was the strength of 400 atomic bombs, it felt as if we were all drowning in an energy tsunami." Very few people know of or consider the devastating effects natural disasters can have on the human body's energy field. People say it will take thirty years to rebuild the inner city of Christchurch. We were there recently, and being sensitive to energy, I am of the opinion healing the shock in people who were in the inner city will also take a long time. All over the world, people are suffering from long term-trauma or shocks that have not been healed on an emotional level. Wars and the shock of 9/11 in the United States have affected whole nations. Many people do not know how to heal energy or that it can and should be healed to avoid long-term emotional and physical ailments.

Write Your Story:

- Can you name a fear situation when you took flight?
- Write down what happened and how you felt while you were fleeing the situation.

Being A *Flighter* Can Make You A Victim

> *"Do not kid yourself; a conflict is never about the surface issue. It's about ones unsaid, untreated, and unhealed wounds."*
>
> — Author Unknown

How often do you feel people take advantage of you and you are helpless to do anything about the situation?

I worked with a client who realised during the *ME* course she was a *Flighter*. She hated conflict and said she was a pleaser. She acknowledged pleasing others was her reaction to fear, and it was easier for her to be the victim than to stand up for herself. I call that a *poisonous pleaser* because you become so filled up with suppressed feelings you start to poison yourself and those around you. She was by nature a sweet and kind person and liked to serve people, but she found people started to expect it of her and abused her kindness. She had to learn to set boundaries and speak up for herself — in a kind and gentle way.

Write Your Story:

- Do you feel you are sometimes in positions where people take advantage of you, but you cannot stand up to them?
- Write down what happens and how you feel when you have all that suppressed poison on the inside.

The Busy-Ness Of Business

> *"The most important place for conflict is a meeting."*
>
> — Author Unknown

Flighters can sometimes struggle with commitment. They say "No" before you have even finished asking a question. On a lighter note, *Flighters* can be recognised in the office as those who never, or seldom, answer when you phone them, are always too busy to see you, and if you track them down in the passage, will say, "I must run to my next meeting." They are the procrastinators in life, always postponing or finding excuses not to do something.

I have a wonderful slide about meetings. It starts with the questions "Are you lonely? Had enough of working alone? Do you hate making decisions?" The solution, "Go to a meeting. There you can meet people, create flip-charts, feel important, impress your colleagues, and drink coffee, all during working time!" The slide ends with "Meetings — the practical alternative to work." Although it is over the top, it always lightens the feeling during a course.

Write Your Story:

- Do you know a *Flighter* or do you fall into this category yourself?
- Write down what you do when you react to fear as a *Flighter*, or if you know others who are *Flighters*, how you feel when dealing with them.

Flighters Influencing Companies And Organisations

> *"When people feel their contributions are not appreciated they will stop trying, and when that happens innovation dies."*
>
> — Mark Sanborn, The Fred Factor

Are you working for a company or boss who motivates employees through fear?

One of our basic emotional needs is to feel appreciated or acknowledged. A story has circulated for years about babies who died in an orphanage without evidence of being sick during World War II. It was only when a matron who picked them up and hugged and cuddled them came to the orphanage that the doctors realised the deaths stopped. After much deliberation, they concluded the babies died due to lack of love through being ignored.

Our need for recognition and appreciation does not stop when we grow up. From my experience working with recognition programmes in companies, the need for recognition is one of the most neglected and misunderstood issues in the corporate world.

I am always amazed how easily companies restructure and lay people off to save money. Anyone with an awareness of the power and energy in words knows that words like "downsizing" and "restructuring" are fear words. The fear in a company definitely rises when those words are mentioned.

"Go slow" is a fear reaction. People keep their heads down, and during times of fear, innovation or continuous improvement cannot flourish. Unfortunately, very few companies or organisations do anything to teach people about reactions to fear or to give them the skills to work productively during times of change. One way to measure the "wellness" in a company or organisation is to look at the sick leave. A fear-motivated place will have a high turnover with sick people or people leaving the company. I have worked with many people who have been made redundant (another fear word), and that fear stays with them, causing havoc in their lives, unless they get help to change their thinking patterns.

Write Your Story:
- Have you been through fear-filled situations in your work as described above?
- Write down whether you had help to get rid of the shock and fear or how you dealt with the situation.

Summary
Being a *Flighter* and trying to keep the peace at all costs happens to many people, especially in work situations where they are afraid. In an effort to bring light into fear-filled companies, I invented the fear bus as a vehicle to take a journey of awareness. Shame, blame, and guilt are the luggage we all bring with us on the fear journey. It is always a good idea to talk to someone who can help you work through your fear, and if you cannot do that, write down your fears and put them in a pot to get distance, and hopefully, perspective.

In a fearful situation, we sometimes laugh — even when facing death. It can be easier to be a victim than to stand up for ourselves. *Flighters* often struggle with commitment and, therefore, avoid making decisions or become very creative to avoid any involvement. Fear words in companies can have a devastating effect on employee morale.

The Biggest Lessons

People who choose to take flight in a fear situation will try to keep the peace at all costs. Keeping quiet and suppressing your words can lead to victimhood and you poisoning your own life. It helps to write down your problems to get distance and look at them from another perspective. Energy fields in the body can get disrupted when emotions are suppressed and can cause physical illness if left unattended.

Word Reveal And The Power Of Words

In the word *Flighters*, the fear words are grief, fret, and flight. *Flighters* can feel insecure, nervous, and trapped. They will blame others because they feel shame and guilt just like *Frighters* and because they want to keep the peace at all cost and have to learn to speak their truth instead of trying to keep everybody happy. Suppressing your feelings and always serving others in order to feel good or get recognition can make you feel like a victim and slowly poison your body. Here are some words revealed in *poisonous pleaser*: asleep, ease, seal, real, release, please, see, soon, reap, our, ear, leap, and peel. The sentence can be: When we awake from being *asleep* and *release our poison*, we *soon please* with *ease* and *reap real pleasure*.

Rainbow Blessing

Thank you for giving me the strength to speak my truth with ease in peaceful ways.

"If we understood the power of our thoughts, we would guard them more closely. If we understood the awesome power of our words, we would prefer silence to almost anything negative. In our thoughts and words, we create our own weaknesses and our own strengths. Our limitations and joys begin in our hearts. We can always replace negative with positive."
— Betty Eadie

Chapter 4 — Fighting: A Fear Reaction To Survive

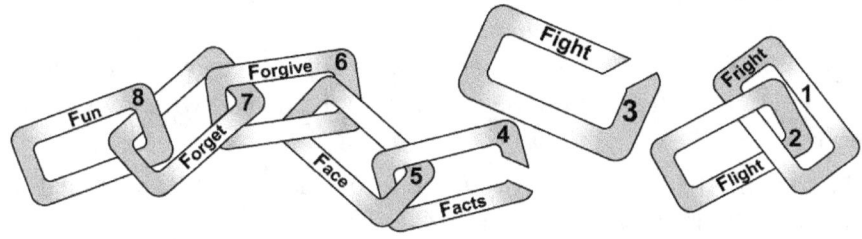

*"Sometimes the strongest among us are the ones who smile
through silent pain, cry behind closed doors,
and fight battles nobody knows about."*
— Author Unknown

Previously, I discussed *Flighters* and how to recognise this response in yourself or others. In Chapter 4, we are going to take a look at *Fighters*.

The family I was born into andrussell the family I married into mostly choose to be *Fighters*. The fundamental belief in the men of both families are you take care of your family by providing for and protecting them. The women in both families are mostly gentle, kind, and supporting, but not pushovers. After more than four decades of marriage, my husband still walks on the side of the road and opens the car door for me, and I appreciate it every time he does, seeing it as him protecting and caring for me.

Learning To Fight Starting With My Brother

*"Whenever you are confronted with an opponent,
conquer him with love."*
— Mahatma Gandhi

Can you remember your first fight with a sibling?

At the age of four, my brother Jack was my best friend and my hero, but also the one person who knew how to make me angry. One day, we were playing with marbles, but there was a wonderful "shooter" (the biggest one) that he did not want to give to me. My mom was sitting nearby, clicking away with her knitting needles. She heard how I was pleading with Jack for a chance to play with the big marble, and how he refused and started to tease me with it. Suddenly, I jumped up, pulled up the sleeves of my red jersey, and said to him, "If you are a man, stand up and fight." The next moment, Jack jumped up and with joy shouted to my mom, "She can fight!"

At eight, that was Jack's criteria for a cool sister! I got the big marble and a brotherly hug. I learned a lesson that day that stayed with me for life. If you are ready to fight for something, you may win without going into the fight.

Write Your Story:

* Can you still remember your first fight?
* Write what you learned in your first fight that stayed with you your whole life.

Fighting Against A System Of Fear

"A teacher's influence writes on the pages of your heart."
— Author Unknown

How do you feel about corporal punishment? Did you grow up in a time when it was still allowed and practised?

I believe every person in my life is a teacher. My mom was one of the best teachers I had. She was also seen by her students in school as a good teacher, and even as adults, whenever they saw Mom, they would always come to her with wonderful stories of how she had influenced their lives in positive ways.

I had a few great teachers, but also teachers who were difficult to get along with. In those days, it was common practice to discipline a child with a spanking in front of the class. To me, that was a cruel way to treat any child. Whenever anyone got punished, I had a hard time not showing my anger, although I was seldom the one on the receiving end of the stick.

One day, I was relating an incident from school to my mom. She told me in her day it had been much worse, so she had made a decision never to punish children that way. In the farming communities in my mother's time, during the Great Depression, people were poor. Most children had to work on the farm after school to help their parents. Having no electricity back then meant they had to study by candlelight at night, with no help from parents who were often illiterate themselves. The words my mom said stayed with me: "I have never found a grownup person who said to me that they are a better person because someone gave them a hiding when they were a child. Most people grow up with bitterness in their souls."

I know many people today think children have no manners or respect because spanking is not allowed anymore. To me, punishing someone like that only caused fear, and it was definitely not the answer.

Write Your Story:

- Did you grow up in a time when people still believed the best way to discipline a child was with a good spanking?
- Maybe you were punished in other ways, leaving you with emotional scars.
- Write how you felt when you were punished and whether it helped or hurt you?

"Competing" Is An Acceptable Fear-Filled Word

"Being second is to be the first of the ones who lose."
— Ayrton Senna

Since my family members do not give up easily (*Fighters*), we are also very competitive. While dealing with my depression, I realised my competitiveness was one of the reasons I suffered from burnout. I always say the ego, which for me is our shadow part, is too eager when it comes to competition. I am in total agreement with George Leonard who said, "Competition is the spice of sports, but if you make spice the whole meal, you'll be sick." It happens all too often that children and grownups collapse under pressure because their egos get the better of them in competition. Competition is still promoted as good, but perhaps it should be seen as having the potential to be a fear motivator.

Confucius said, "The will to win, the desire to succeed, the urge to reach your full potential…these are the keys that will unlock the door to personal excellence." In Chapter 13, I will write more about excellence and the influence it had on my life. Personally, I agree that excellence is not being the best — it is doing your best. T. S. Eliot said, "Excellence encourages one about life generally; it shows the spiritual wealth of the world." I do not think competing in anything brings out the spiritual part in a person. The words "competing against" invoke emotions of fear in many people and cause a "fear reaction."

Write Your Story:

- Do you like to compete against yourself or other people?
- Write down your typical feelings before you compete in any event.

Fighting In The Workplace

Fighting is all about control and power, with anger as a reaction when experiencing opposition. This statement sums it up nicely for me — not just for *Fighters* in their private life but also at work. Most of us on the *fear bus* have heard phrases like "Fight for what you want" or "Life is tough; you have to fight for what you want."

Below are examples of *Fighters*. Can you identify with some of the examples or identify similar people in your family or workplace? Interestingly, *Fighters* are often the leaders in a community or working environment.

Fighters have to be in control. Depending on many factors, they can use all kinds of methods to keep control of the people or situations they manage. They can be masters in manipulation, even going to the extremes of rudeness, making people feel ashamed in order to be in power.

Write Your Story:

- Are you responsible in your home life or working environment for people acting like *Fighters*?
- Write down what you do as a *Fighter* or how you feel dealing with *Fighters* in your everyday life.

Stepping Over The Line Into Aggression

Do you get angry or frustrated easily?

After working through my own depression as a *Frighter* and then dealing with the suppression of my feelings as a *Flighter*, I had to face my anger as a *Fighter*. With the knowledge and experience of working through my anger, and in my capacity as a facilitator and teacher for self-discovery, I have helped many people through the years to understand and deal with their anger.

Angry people, no matter whether they are children or grownups, always have a feeling of helplessness beneath their anger. Road rage is a wonderful example of our helplessness coming to the front. The person who irritates us on the road is seldom aware of our frustration. Because our cars give us a false feeling of power and control, we show our anger to strangers, but most of the time, the irritation or frustration was already in us. When I work with people who overreact in such situations, I ask them whether they can get past blaming the other person and acknowledge the anger is in them; then I ask them to go through the anger and feel the emotion underneath. They always respond their underlying emotion is one of feeling helpless. Aggressive people who are abusive often feel as helpless as the people they are abusing.

I have watched toddlers in day care centres and noticed how their frustration built when they could not play outside due to rainy weather. One of their favourite ways to get rid of their frustration is to bite their friends. Unfortunately for them, that behaviour cannot be allowed, and they learn quickly about the results of their "wrong" choices. The domestication process teaches us from a young age about guilt and shame. Another interesting observation I had was children wearing red clothing were more inclined to aggressive behaviour. When I spoke to teachers where the school's formal uniform was red, the teachers were very surprised when I told them the colour of the school uniform probably had a big influence on the students' aggressive behaviour!

Write Your Story:

- Do you abuse people or even harm yourself due to a feeling of helplessness?
- Write down how you are going to work with this reaction to fear.

Pushing Back

Do you react negatively when people give you advice, such as changing your lifestyle even if it is for your own benefit?

We all have a built-in, push-back mechanism. Physically or emotionally, when we feel pushed, we will react by pushing back.

During my training as facilitator for Investment in Excellence, our facilitator, Mr Smith, asked one of the students to put his hand against Mr Smith's hand. Mr Smith slightly increased the pressure in his own hand and immediately the student pushed back. When Mr Smith asked why the student pushed him, the answer was "You pushed me first." I still use this example to demonstrate to people how easy it is to push back when you feel you are being pushed. When it happens on an emotional level, we can get all kinds of reactions. People "go slow" or even do more of the same thing. For example, people not heeding warnings or recommendations when advised by a doctor or a friend to eat healthy foods, will eat more unhealthy food or not heed the warning at all. The question we should ask ourselves: "Is my eating an addiction, or am I giving 'push back' because I feel someone wants to control me or tell me what to do and that makes me feel helpless?" Our bodies give us "push back" when we have pain or a physical illness.

Write Your Story:

- Can you remember a situation when you reacted to feeling pushed?
- If so, write down what you did and why.

Training Yourself And Your Mind Can Save Your Life

Do you know how you react to fear?

I have been a *Frighter*, *Flighter*, or *Fighter* depending on the situation. I will mostly be a *Flighter* or *Fighter* and that is a fact I have acknowledged. You have most probably also faced the fact you react as a *Frighter*, *Flighter*, or *Fighter* depending on the situation you face, your personality, and many other factors.

One of my favourite ways to illustrate all three fear reactions is a story my son Brian gave me.

There is a house on fire in your street. *Frighters* will stand inside or outside the house in absolute fear, just staring at the flames or become hysterical. *Flighters* may run away from the flames to safety instead of helping the people on the inside. They may phone for help or keep busy organising in the background. The *Fighter* is the fireman or the person running into the burning house to try to save the people and their belongings. We have to understand that when we react in fear, we do so either by training or instinct, and that will always be our "first" choice. Being trained to handle dangerous situations does not mean we are without fear.

Write Your Story:

- Write down a few fear situations you have been in and whether you reacted the same way every time.

Summary

Learning how to fight and to stand up for myself was a good lesson at the age of four, but there is never an excuse for abusing people or any living being. Abuse is fear motivated and shows the helplessness of the abuser — his or her inability to know how to handle the situation. Competition can cause people to react in fear. While trying to compete, many people can suffer from burnout. The biggest problem is in the workplace, where interactions are often about power and control.

The more helpless we feel, the more anger we can project. If you get pushed too far, you will push back. The same principle is true when it comes to our bodies. Not taking care of our bodies will result in disease — disease happens when we do not feel at ease in our body, which is the body's way of telling us to stop pushing it so hard. Knowing how you react in fearful situations can save your life.

The Biggest Lessons

Fighters can be angry, aggressive people who feel helpless or do not know how to handle situations.

Word Reveal And The Power Of Words

In the word *Fighters*, the fear words are fight and stir. *Fighters* often feel pushed themselves or trapped. They are insecure and nervous, blaming and shaming others because they need to feel in control. They do not want to acknowledge that in certain areas of their lives they are out of control. Like *Frighters* and *Fighters*, they have to learn to manage their energy first, instead of trying to manage and control other people.

Rainbow Blessing

Help me to stay calm and not get scared when I deal with angry people. Let the pink ray of love heal the fear and helplessness in our hearts.

Chapter 5 — Working With Facts

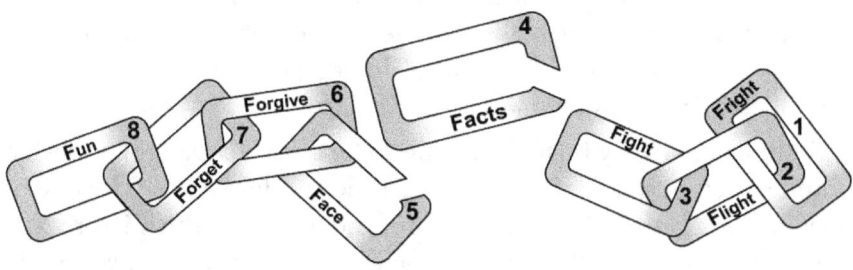

*"All human unhappiness comes from
not facing reality squarely, exactly as it is."*
— Buddha

Having established in the previous chapters we can choose all three, or at least two of the three reactions to fear, depending on the situation we are in, we will now take a look at the first step in working through the process of dealing with fear. Writing how we see our present situation, as we perceive it, is an important step. We always have to keep in mind that perceptions rule our world, but they are not necessarily the truth about the situation.

Facting Is Just A Map — A Starting Point

Are you someone who wants to hear the facts, or do you know someone in your life who says, "Just give me the facts"?

As a child, I liked writing poems and stories. Most of my stories also ended with "And they lived happily ever after", but I did not really know anything about that statement. Finding my own answers on the *fear bus* was almost like building my own happily ever after. One of the first steps I took to discover myself again was to look at the facts of my belief system at that point in my journey on the fear bus. It was an "aha" moment for me as the *word reveal* for "belief system" showed me the following words: is, be, lies, fly, file, it, if, life, flee, bites, my, me. I could make the following sentences out of those words: Is it a lie? My lies bite me; flee if beliefs bite me; and file lies. I asked myself how many lies were in my belief system? Could I file the outdated beliefs or flee from the fear-motivated ones that were all about doing something or else....

The bottom line of "or else" was never a good option on the *fear bus*. Hell and feeling like a sinner were the ultimate punishment. I started to see many of my beliefs were rooted in fear, especially since I was brought up in a very conservative Afrikaans, Christian community with a lot of fear-filled beliefs. I asked myself, "Is my life a lie?"

Somewhere in my busy life trying to be a perfect daughter, perfect homemaker, perfect wife, and perfect mom, I lost myself. I woke up one morning, went into the bathroom, and looked in the mirror. I said to myself, "You are a wife, a mother, a daughter, but who are you?" The face staring at me was that of a young woman who was living a busy life and didn't know the person who was looking at her. I have always been a fact-finding kind of person. Especially during this time, I preferred to work with people who relied on facts and did not become emotional about everything. I turned around and went to my study, took a piece of paper, and started to write down the facts of my life as I saw them at that moment. Below is the list I wrote.

Fact 1: We are born without fear, but get "domesticated" through fear.

Fact 2: I was a "Frighter" when I had depression because I was frozen with fear.

Fact 3: Living in the desert was my "Flighter" reaction to fear.

Fact 4: Most of the time I choose to be a "Fighter" when I am in a fear situation.

Fact 5: I often feel different.

Fact 6: We are unconscious on the "fear bus."

Fact 7: Facing the facts about my life makes me feel more alive and conscious of my reactions in situations.

Fact 8: Fear made me physically sick.

Fact 9: Trying to let my family experience what I am learning is not a good idea.

Fact 10: Some people are trying too hard to live their past to death.

Fact 11: Taking on our patients' problems does not help them. It is our own ego, keeping us important.

Fact 12: Everything you are running away from is in your head. Start tracking or stalking yourself.

Write Your Story:

*   Write down the facts you see as your reality at the moment. Look at the facts without getting too emotional.

Summary

Looking at the facts of what you think and feel at this moment is always a good starting point. We have to remember it is our perceptions, and not necessarily the truth, that rule our world. Remember "belief system" has the word "lies" in it. Ask yourself how many of your beliefs are outdated or not the truth for you anymore.

The Biggest Lessons

Creating a list of facts as you see it at a specific moment can help you discover the lies in your belief system. The emotions we feel due to our perceptions rule our world, but they are not necessarily the truth.

Word Reveal And The Power Of Words

Words in *Belief system* are: is, be, lies, fly, file, it, if, life, flee, bite, my, me. The sentences made me question many of my beliefs, like: Is it a lie? My lies bite me; flee if beliefs bite me; and file lies. How many of us have lived in fear and thought our beliefs are facts, seeing them for the truth? It may serve you well to start questioning your belief system.

Rainbow Blessing

Thank you for the courage to write down the facts in my life.

*"We are all so much together
and yet we are all dying of loneliness."*
— Leo Buscaglia

Chapter 6 — Facing The Facts – Facing Me

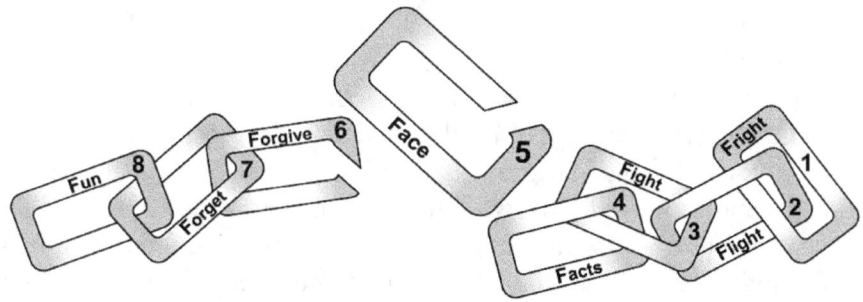

"Facing facts is always empowering."
— Eckhart Tolle

Having determined the facts of where we are, in this chapter, we look at how to move forward with courage.

Showing Courage On The *Fear Bus*

"Anyone can run away; it's super-easy.
Facing problems and working through them,
that's what makes you strong."
— Author Unknown

Facing the facts and dealing with them takes a lot of courage when you are on the *fear bus*. Are you ready to face the facts about your fears?

How often do we say or think, "I am…." I sometimes have a resistance when it comes to saying who I am. As you know by now, I am always looking for the meaning within words, and when I was working with "face" and "facts," I saw the word "facets." We are all like diamonds with many facets, and everything that happens to us is a way of polishing or shaping us so another facet can shine. If I say I am a writer, healer, or coach, the world can file me under those headings. When someone says, "She's a…" or "He's a…" we can tend to take that perception as the truth and start to act as if we are that one facet of ourselves. How many of us are living by a belief that is only a facet of who we are, that may not even be true, but just a reaction to fear.

We take on tags like "I'm fat", "I'm an addict", "I'm a housewife", "I'm a failure", or students will say: "I'm not good in this or that subject"— the list goes on.

My favourite introduction of myself is my version of creation. I like to tell this story because it is lighthearted but has a deeper meaning — that we have the answer to our own "Godness" within us. It is up to every person to find their own light within. "I am a hue man", which means I am a human with colours surrounding me. God made a human being and called it man, which according to my friend Google, means a human being of either sex. Then God decided to add colour, hiding the colours of the rainbow inside the "man" "woman" creation. Looking at the male-female created in our Father-Mother God's image and seeing the beautiful colours inside them, God exclaimed in awe: "Hue Man!"

It is interesting to realise in "Yahweh", which is the proper name of God in the Old Testament, is also the word "awe." This is how we became man and woman. It is the hue hidden within us and surrounding us that makes us awesome creations.

I am on Earth, which, if turned around, is "heart." I believe I have to learn something new every day, and I can say I am living in the University of Earth to learn about love. Being in relationships, I learn to open my heart to love. I think we are all on Earth or in this university of the heart to learn about love. Everybody wants to have a qualification, and since I have thrown mine all away or outgrown them, I like to make people smile by saying my qualification is a QBEE: *Qualified By Earthly Experiences.* I like to think we all have to get a QBEE when in the University of the Heart.

Write Your Story:

- What is your perception of who you are?
- Have you become something or someone who is living out a facet of your fear-filled life that is not the real you?
- Write down who you think you are and what you say to people when they ask you to introduce yourself. Is that really you, or a facet of your life?

Facing Our Addictions On Paper As We Fact Them

"What this generation must do is face its problems."
— John F. Kennedy

Are you ready to take the next step in your healing journey on the fear bus?

It can be a very enlightening experience to face our fears and the facts about our fears. This is where we look at our lives and take responsibility for our circumstances instead of blaming the outside world for our problems. To do that, we have to become aware of what we are thinking and feeling every moment of every day. You need to face the facts about yourself and accept them. This is the beginning of working with ME (My Energy).

In Chapter 2, I touched on addictions and how I learnt a lot about addictive behaviour during my depression. Addictive personalities do not have control over what they are doing, taking, or using. Addictions spiraling out of control quickly reach a point where they are harmful to addicts and their families. Addictions are not just to physical things we consume, such as drugs or alcohol, but also include behaviours, such as gambling or addictions to seemingly harmless products, like chocolate or coffee — in other words, addiction may refer to a substance dependence (e.g. drug addiction) or behavioural addiction (e.g. gambling addiction).

In the past, addictions meant the use of psychoactive substances crossing the blood-brain barrier, temporarily altering the chemical balance of the brain, which included alcohol, tobacco, and some drugs. Today, psychologists, health care professionals, and lay people insist psychological dependency, as may be the case with gambling, sex, internet usage, work, exercise, food, etc., should also be counted as addictions because they all lead to feelings of guilt, shame, hopelessness, despair, failure, rejection, anxiety, and/or humiliation.

I say these are all fear-filled words. When people are addicted to something, they cannot control how they use it and become dependent on their drug of choice. An addiction is a form of escape from facing the facts of what you do with your energy and how you handle stress.

Facing the truth about someone or something means you have to acknowledge and accept the consequences. To see the fact on a piece of paper and to accept the truth about yourself even if it is undesirable takes a lot of courage, but it is a starting point on the healing journey.

Write Your Story:

- What do you do to avoid facing the truth about your life? As quickly as you can, write down the facts about that problem.

- Take about five minutes and do not give a lot of thought to this. Just write down the facts as they come into your mind.

- Do not get emotional about it. They are only facts about the situation, neither good nor bad.

Facing Our Shadow

> *"The ego is the false self — born out of fear and defensiveness."*
> — John O'Donohue

Did you ever try to outrun your shadow as a child?

My mother had five sisters, and growing up on a farm in the Kenhardt district (a very remote part of South Africa) they had to entertain themselves. One of their favourite "games" on windy days was to find tumbleweed and throw it into the wind. The one who could outrun the rolling "ball" was free from chores or watching the smaller children for the day.

On days when they had no wind, they tried to outrun their own shadows. What fun I had trying to outrun a tumbleweed as a child. Trying to outrun my own shadow was impossible. This little story taught me a valuable lesson. I see the ego as my shadow. Our shadow is not something we look at every day. And yet it is always with us even if we cannot see it. We know and accept we have a shadow and mostly ignore it.

Growing up, I learnt that your shadow could give you a good indication of the time during the day. It always impressed me when our friends, Peter and Ellen, who were our best playmates on the farm, could look at the position of the sun or our shadows and tell what time of day it was. Watching the sun going down and our shadows getting longer was not seen by us as a sign to stop playing. Many an evening we got into trouble as we kept playing after my mother told them it was time to go home. Long after sunset, they would run home. We could only see two little heads bobbing through the fields, while we hoped for their sakes their mom was busy somewhere behind the house when they slipped in through the front door.

I like to tell the story of how we looked at our shadows as children when teaching people that our ego is like our shadow. Our ego is not really who we are, but we sometimes forget who we really are — and the more we live in fear, the more we follow our shadow on the fear bus. Likening our ego to our shadows, it is easy to see how the ego can "overshadow" us as we live from ego or shadow instead of our authentic self. Facing our fear is like facing our shadow.

Our fear is nothing unless we give it power through our thoughts, feelings, words, and actions. Sometimes we are trying too hard to outrun our past. If we realise the past is but a shadow that we cannot outrun, we can be in the present, accepting that shadow or past experience that may have been traumatic. We can surrender into the moment and let go of past hurts.

Write Your Story:
- Are you tired of running after your shadow?
- What does your ego make you do that is not who you are just to get attention?
- Write about the shadow you are trying to outrun.

Shadowing Makes Us Feel Important

"I am stressed about work." I am stressed about exams." "I am worried about my patients." "I am scared I will let someone down." "I am tired of working late." "What will happen if I lose the game or do poorly in school?" Have you heard any of these statements before? Are you saying something similar?

The ego works for attention. I have stated before that showing appreciation is important. Not only for humans, but all living beings respond positively when appreciated. On the fear bus, many people still have to learn self-appreciation or self-love, and therefore, they look for appreciation outside themselves. It does not really matter if we get negative attention, as long as we get attention.

I have worked for more than thirty years in the field of self-empowerment and self-healing. In all walks of life, I have heard people say the words with which I started my story. No matter what profession you're in — whether you're a doctor, teacher, alternative healer, student, parent — you likely suffer from this fear-based sickness of worry and stress. To worry about someone or something is the ego making you feel or look important. It is not helping the other person. An overworked or stressed-out government official, doctor, healer, church official, mother, or father can be of no value to anybody. We have to ask ourselves why we keep doing this. The only answer I can come up with is it makes us feel important. Today, children in schools get "shadowed" by a teacher as punishment for bad behaviour. I am sure many of the kids find that reassuring for keeping their little egos intact.

Write Your Story:
- What are you doing, or which words are you using, to keep your ego feeling important?
- Write down words you use to fit in with the crowd on your *fear bus*.

Tracking Yourself

> *"You cannot change what you don't manage;*
> *you cannot manage what you don't track."*
> — Valentino Crawford

Have you ever watched a cat stalking its prey?

I love the Toltec way of living, so I appreciate Don Miguel Ruiz, an author of Toltec spiritual teachings, saying we have to learn "stalking" ourselves. Having grown up near the Kalahari in South Africa, I have an affinity with the Bushmen and the way they can track an animal for days. Tracking our own thoughts, feelings, words, and actions with patience and dedication like the Bushmen following an animal is my way of understanding the process.

Recently, I found a new way of describing what tracking really is. GPS stands for global positioning system, and most of us, at least those in big cities or who travel a lot, have a GPS. Now there is an internal GPS receiver on the market. Its description says it collects location data from satellites circling the earth. To break free of the fear thoughts repeating and circling in our minds every day, we need to use our internal GPS and start tracking our thoughts, feelings, words, and actions. Facing the facts about our fears means becoming aware or mindful of them and realising everything we are running away from happens inside our heads.

Write Your Story:

- Switch on your internal GPS and write down some of the thoughts, feelings, and words you receive from your internal system for the next five minutes.

- Start with only five minutes and then repeat the exercise a few times, gradually increasing the time as you get used to the feedback from your ME GPS (MY Energy GPS).

- You can do this exercise on a separate piece of paper or in the specific book you keep for awakening your energy.

Facing Facts In The Workplace

"When dealing with people, remember you are not dealing with creatures of logic, but creatures of emotion."
— Dale Carnegie

Have you ever heard these words in your workplace? "Don't get emotional. See the facts."

Sadly, too many fear-motivated workplaces do not realise the truth of the Dale Carnegie quote above. There is very little space for emotions in the work environment. Knowing about fear reactions, I always find it interesting to watch people at work. The *Frighters* and the *Flighters* will mostly be quiet in meetings, but they will have their own meeting afterwards, either with themselves or by telling others who will listen what they think. Adam S. McHugh said, "When introverts are in conflict with each other...it may require a map in order to follow all the silences, nonverbal cues, and passive-aggressive behaviours!"

I like to use techniques showing people that even if they think they have all the facts, they may not — they do not see all the Fs. Read the sentence below just once and then count all the Fs you see in words.

"Finished files are the result of years of scientific study combined with the experience of many years of experts."

Most people reading the sentence will count three or four Fs the first time. There are seven Fs. When people do this exercise and realise it is easy to miss an "F", they start to cooperate and work together.

I first did this exercise in my Investment in Excellence course. It opened my eyes and resulted in writing my own course with nine Fs: fear, fright, flight, fight, facts, and face, forgive, forget, and fun. I call it the *fear chain*.

When you are on the *fear bus*, your reactions to fear can become like a chain you are dragging behind you. That chain is keeping you from living a life of happiness. So many people in management positions cannot handle conflict and will do anything in their power to eliminate its source. I have seen people made redundant because of managers who were too afraid of conflict or did not know how to handle it. Robert Townsend sums it up like this: "A good manager doesn't try to eliminate conflict; he tries to keep it from wasting the energies of his people. If you're the boss and your people fight you openly when they think that you are wrong, that's healthy."

Write Your Story:

- Can you name a few fear-filled people in your workplace?
- Write down how you react to fear in your working environment.

Summary

We have many facets, so we have to be careful not to live our profession as if it is our true self. Facing the facts about ourselves and accepting them is the beginning of managing our energy. Addictions keep us in fear and are a form of escape from facing the truth about ourselves.

Our shadow part is our ego, and it wants attention. Switching on our internal GPS to track and follow our own progress will bring more clarity to who we are. Facing the facts about fear in the workplace can build a formidable workforce.

The Biggest Lessons

Taking responsibility for our circumstances instead of blaming others means we have to learn to be watchful of our thoughts, feelings, words, and actions all the time.

Word Reveal And The Power Of Words

The words *Face* and *Facts* give you *Facets*. In *Blame* is *lame* and *me*. It will benefit the *Blamers* to realise it is *lame* to *blame me*.

Rainbow Blessing

I bless those who are brave enough to face their fears and addictions and to discover all the facets of their lives.

"Love builds bridges where there are none."
— R.H. Delaney

Chapter 7 — Forgiving: The Twin Of Forgetting

"Forgiveness has nothing to do with absolving a criminal of his crime. It has everything to do with relieving oneself of the burden of being a victim — letting go of the pain and transforming oneself from victim to survivor."

— C. R. Strahan

In the last two chapters, we saw that *facing the facts* about ourselves and our beliefs and perceptions is the first step in moving away from a life lived in fear. In the next two chapters, we will focus on *Forgiving* and *Forgetting*.

Unveiling the word Forgive (Word Reveal)

Forgive — Grief, Rife, Forge, Fire, Five, Or, Ogre. Let us take each word and look at its meaning.

Forgiving Myself

"To forgive is to set a prisoner free and discover that the prisoner was you."

— Lewis B. Smedes

Do you know most of your suffering happens in your mind?

Grief — If you are in a situation where there is no forgiveness, is it true to say that you can suffer grief?

Forgive and Forget are the twins in the *fear chain*. You cannot do one without the other. Everything that happens to us (if not dealt with properly) can escalate into emotional energy blocks and cause physical disease. Depending on the situation, one or both parties may apologise, but the emotional pain persists, and depending on the issue, can go on for years with terrible physical and emotional effects. As stated earlier, when we are not at ease with our lives, we get disease. Fear-filled words like stress, abuse, and trauma are common in our vocabulary.

In the early days on my *fear bus*, I realised there were not many people I had to forgive, but I had a lot to work through in forgiving myself. Today, I still do the mirror exercise, which I learnt from Louise Hay, by myself and with others. You stand in front of a mirror or hold one up, and you look at yourself — really look into your eyes. You ask your soul, your mind, and your body to forgive you for abusing them in so many ways every day. Many people have so much self-loathing they cannot even look in the mirror.

In the early 1990s, I was working with a wonderful spiritual therapist, Melissa. At the time, I had so much grief in me from blocking off my emotions for a long time. I felt I could not cry, because if I did, I would begin with the misinterpretations that started with Adam and Eve — I would mourn the fact Christ was crucified 2000 years ago, but we still drag sin out from behind every bush. I would cry right through the world wars. Cry for all the suffering, pain, and death. I would cry for every man, woman, and child who suffers pain or abuse. I was afraid that if I cried, I would not be able to stop the well of tears buried deep inside me for so long.

However, the pain I felt eventually became greater than my fear, so I booked a therapy session with Melissa, telling her I would like to cry. I cried for two hours while that lovely woman held my hand and just sat there silently, holding me in loving energy. I opened my heart and cried for all the years I had tried so hard to be perfect. I cried as many thoughts came into my mind. I felt the feelings I had not allowed. I cried as words spoken and unspoken drifted through me — and when there were no more tears in my well of grief, I got up and went home.

I felt sick from all the crying, but there was a lightness of being that came and stayed with me from that day on.

Never underestimate the healing power of a good therapist. Melissa did a lot of work with me for a long time, and that day, without saying a word, she held me in the loving energy I so needed.

Forgiving others is sometimes easier than forgiving yourself. Don't be afraid to ask for help when you work through your fear reactions. Being a Fighter and thinking it is weak to cry was only one way my ego made me feel important. It gave me a false sense of power and control. Tears are the soul's water used to clean your heart.

I did not have such a hard time forgiving those who hurt me, but it was hard to face the fact most of my hurt and pain were in my own mind and I allowed it to almost destroy me. I love this quote from Tony Robbins: "Forgiveness is a gift you give yourself." Indeed, allowing the tears helped me receive the gift of forgiving myself.

Write Your Story:

- Have you forgiven yourself?

  People's first reaction when I ask this question is either "I don't know how" or "I have done nothing wrong."

  Remember, forgiveness does not excuse your or other people's bad behaviour, but it stops bad behaviour from destroying your life. David Ridge says it very appropriately: "True forgiveness is not an act after the fact; it is an attitude with which you enter each moment."

- Write down how you feel after forgiving yourself. If you are too scared to do this exercise on your own, please see my contact particulars at the end of this book or contact someone you trust to help you.

Forgiving Is A Universal Lesson

> *"If I could learn to treat triumph and disaster the same,*
> *then I would find bliss."*
> — Kathie Lee Gilford

Can you imagine a world where there is no fighting, pain, or abuse of any kind?

Rife — Some of the synonyms for the word rife, which hides in the word forgive, are common, extensive, and widespread. Looking at the extensive and ongoing abuse that is prevalent in our fear-filled world, it is safe to say forgiveness is a common, universal lesson, and we all have to learn to deal with it if we want to change the world into a safe place. I look at the faces of children in the war-torn countries — surrounded by fear, death, hatred, and so many fear-filled thoughts, feelings, and words. Many little faces stare at the camera without any emotion. Frozen little statues, another lost generation, the legacy of leaders who use people for their own benefit. In their world where fear and darkness are the only way of living — these children know — love, light, trust, and joy are non-existent. The following story came to me as I looked at a picture of a child from a war-torn country.

Riyadh ran into the dark cave. For a few moments, he stood in the darkness, every muscle in his thin, little body tensed as he listened for the sound of approaching danger from outside, or worse, from inside the cave. Five minutes passed. His eyes were getting used to the darkness. His breathing was back to normal. Nothing moved inside the cave. He could not hear the gunfire anymore, but the smell of death was still on his clothes. For days, they had been running, hiding, with very little water and no food. They ran to escape the fighting following them like a hungry predator.

An hour earlier, he had woken amidst total chaos. The terror living inside him — his constant companion — almost choked him to death. All around him, people were shouting and running. Dead and wounded people were everywhere. Riyadh did not think. He just ran, every moment expecting to be killed. It was only when he stumbled into the cave that he realised he was alive and safe.

He slumped down onto the floor of the cave and slept. The next day, he started to walk toward the border, hoping he remembered the way. He had tried to listen to the grownups in the group. There were seven of them, all trying to get to the border and safety. Riyadh's parents had died a few weeks before when their village was caught in the crossfire between soldiers and rebels.

After two days, Riyadh reached the border, dehydrated and on the verge of collapse.

Riyadh's story had a good ending. He was rescued and flown to another country where he was adopted by a loving couple who had three children of their own. It took a long time for this little boy to understand the world of death and destruction he left behind was in his past. His new family told him how to observe his thoughts, feel the feelings of loss, anger, grief, and sadness, but not to get caught up in those feelings and thoughts. They taught him how to sweep the thoughts from his mind, to clear the space by forgiving the people who had wronged him in so many ways, and to find positive and loving words to replace all the fear words he was carrying in his mind.

Riyadh made a list of all those fear words, and opposite every fear word he wrote a love word. It took him a long time to change his thoughts and feelings from fear to love, but he did it. He became a young man, and today, he is helping children from the country where he lost everything, but his life, to heal and open their hearts again. He is teaching them that sometimes we get caught up in places of fear and darkness so we can learn and appreciate how forgiveness opens us up to a world of love, peace, and joy.

Riyadh believes as more people live in love and spread light over the world, the leaders who still want to control people through war and fear will be overthrown and there will come a day when we will have peace on Earth.

Write Your Story:

- Have you been in a situation where you had to fight for your life?
- Write down what happened and ask yourself whether you have worked on forgiveness in this situation.

Forge — an interesting word hidden in forgive — a forge can be a special fireplace where form takes shape by beating or hammering. It is also a concentrated effort. Forgiving, or rather unforgiving, can feel like being in a very warm place where you get hammered over and over until you are able to understand the importance of forgive and forget. Oprah Winfrey sums it up very nicely: "True forgiveness is when you can say thank you for that experience."

Holding on to grievances and not forgiving can feel like hell. Now that is a word associated with fire! Roberto Assagioli said: "Without forgiveness life is governed by an endless cycle of resentment and retaliation."

Forgiveness does not happen by itself. It is, in my experience, always a concentrated effort to change your attitude from one of unforgiveness to living forgiveness.

Looking at the story of Riyadh, we can admit that he was in a "forge" while living in a war-torn country, but with help and by taking action, he changed his attitude and as such changed his whole perception of his world.

Write Your Story:

* Did you go through a time when it felt as if you were in a furnace and getting hammered until you could forgive and realise it all happened to open you up to becoming whole or healed from your unforgiving nature?
* Write down your version of your experience being in your own "hell."

Five — This number in forgive took me back to Linda Goodman's book *Star Signs* in which she wrote the following on the meaning of the Five Vibration:

Change is the never-ending necessity for 5-people. Change of scene, change in relationships, residence, spiritual and political beliefs. It is difficult for a 5-person to submit to the feelings and the intuition, the intellect is determined to find logical answers...love is made of instinct and feelings, not logic....

What caught my eye in the description of the number five was the word "change." Indeed, when you can let go of trying to analyse everything with your mind and open your heart to forgive yourself and others, it is not only your life that changes but your whole world.

Or — this little word gives us choice. We can poison ourselves by being unforgiving and holding on to old grievances, or we can let go and forgive.

Ogre — This interesting word in forgive is defined in the dictionary as a "man-eating monster, one whose sternness inspires fear." Are we man-eating monsters in our own lives or the lives of other people because we cling to unforgiveness out of fear? Not forgiving can be the fear motivator causing us to carry on hating ourselves and others for years. Are you unforgiving because you do not know how to fill the void if you cannot hate, be angry, or be a victim anymore? Riyadh's story leaves us with a little hope that future generations in war-torn countries can rehabilitate themselves. Those people live in a world of fear, and no matter how much the rest of the world wants to help, they themselves must realise what they have created and start to create something new.

Nelson Mandela was an example of forgiveness for the world. He summed it up as follows: "As I walked out the door toward the gate that would lead to my freedom, I knew if I didn't leave my bitterness and hatred behind, I'd still be in prison." Nelson Mandela went to prison as an angry, unforgiving, fighting terrorist. He could have taken revenge when he was released, and then South Africa would have ended up like many other African countries in a state of ongoing war. Instead, he changed his attitude and a whole country learnt about forgiveness. Unfortunately, his successors chose greed, corruption, and discrimination, which is also fear-based, thus ruining Mandela's wonderful legacy of forgiveness and love.

To forgive is not easy. Forgiving the one who caused your pain can be more painful than the wounds that person inflicted upon you. And yet it is the only way to peace. Forgiveness sets us free.

Write Your Story:

- Many people live in countries with leaders in need of forgiveness for what they have done to their people.
- Write the story of what you have to forgive your leaders for.

Taking Our Luggage With Us Through Life

How much luggage have you brought with you on your *fear bus*?

One of my favourite sayings is there can be no love where there is shame, blame, or guilt.

Let's look at the definitions of these three words. Blame means to think, feel, or say a person or thing is responsible for something bad. Other words for blame are guilt, fault, and responsibility. I would like to remind you the opposite of blame can be happiness, absolution, or forgiveness. I will write about uplifting words later in this book. All we must remember in this chapter is that blame needs forgiveness.

Shame is a feeling of guilt, regret, humiliation, distress, or sadness you have because you know you have done something wrong or behaved foolishly. We can replace the word shame with disgrace, dishonour, and humiliation. On the positive side, we have honour and glory. I am giving you the positive words so you may feel the higher energy vibration as you read.

Guilt is a feeling of responsibility or remorse, whether real or imaginary, for having done something wrong that is against the law. I have said before the brain works for the truth as it perceives it — imaginary or real. We all know that feeling of shame, regret, worry, or unhappiness you have when you have done something wrong. The fact of being found guilty and being held responsible for the humiliation of what happened can be devastating. The word guilt can be replaced by remorse, blame, or responsibility. I love the opposite word — innocence.

I stopped my *fear bus* and took out the luggage I had in the back. I opened my heart and mind as I would open a suitcase. I had a colourful suitcase filled with the different layers of clothes I used as masks to cover my feelings over the years.

I looked at the layers of blame. The first "garment" I found in my luggage was a red anger mask to blame others for causing me to be angry. I looked at that mask and realised even if I dropped it, I still had anger in me. The people on the outside had nothing to do with my anger. I had to take the blaming virus out of my own mind and forgive myself for blaming others. Underneath my anger, I found layers of helplessness, and I realised underneath our anger we feel helpless most of the time. There was a dark orange cloak for the days when I tried too hard to prove my self-worth. I pulled out the dark yellow jacket I wore during my depression to cover the fact I felt guilty. There was a yellow-green skirt that I liked to wear to cover my fear.

As I worked through the layers and took each layer out of my mind to look at it, I let go of my feelings of victimhood — all the shame and regret about things I had done or did not do. There are so many layers of fear. Having been stripped by my own thoughts and feelings of inadequacy, and of my own power, I hid behind those layers of very unbecoming clothing. I had to take out dark blue layers for my conservatism and judgemental attitude towards myself and others. I shed the layers of fear as I opened a well of unshed tears that washed my gaping wounds.

Forgiveness changed my focus physically and energetically. I left the desert road with its long, weary hours of shocks and sadness and walked into the new paradise where I could create a beautiful new reality. I accepted my shadow part was the only thing that was with me all the time. It was not shouting any more in my mind. The guilt virus was quiet. I knew we are all in the University of Heart (University of Earth) where we live and learn about fear and love as the duality on the same bus. I celebrated my new awareness and the freedom of finding the balance on my journey, knowing about my luggage, and choosing to leave the fear garments behind. It took me a long time to unlearn all the layers I put on to cover my innocence.

Write Your Story:

- Would you like to stop your fear bus and take out your luggage of shame, blame, and guilt?
- Write down what you would like to leave behind.
- To make it a fun exercise, write down the colours of layers you take off.

Motivating The World With Fear

The mind works for the truth as it perceives it. Fear motivation works. It works all over the world. When we are children, we learn to do something or else there will be consequences. When I was in school, my fear motivation was that I had to do my homework and get good grades or else I could not get into college or university. The "or else" was not an option for a *fighter* like me since that spelt failure. In college, I had to study in order to get a decent job. Once again, the opposite was having no job and not being able to support myself or a family. That was an unthinkable option. I had always thought I would have arrived after I had finished school and college and landed myself a very nice job.

Then I found myself in relationships. I learnt quickly you behave in a certain way or else…you end up alone. In society, I was expected to abide by certain rules or else I was up against the law. In religion, I had to conduct myself according to the religious laws or else I would go to hell. By the time I was in my twenties, I did not need people to tell me what to do. My brain was trained with shame and blame.

Looking at my luggage on the *fear bus*, I realised shame and blame both ended in guilt. If you blame yourself constantly, it leads to the victim status of shame and the worm of guilt lives in your mind forever. That guilt virus becomes a living thing in your mind, keeping you in fear, resulting in struggle and scarcity as it invades or takes over your life.

It is sometimes easier to blame something or someone outside ourselves for the misery of our lives. One of the lessons I had to learn was forgiveness does not automatically lead to a healed relationship. If you are unforgiving, you attract people into your life who are also unforgiving. Working with forgiveness, it is good to know there are people who may not be capable of love. They will walk out of your life. It is better to let them go along with your anger and blame.

In South Africa, we often use the word shame to express sentimental pleasure, especially at something small and endearing. If someone relates a story and we want to sympathise with them, we will say, "Shame, I am so sorry to hear you were sick" or "Shame, look at the poor hungry little kitten."

I have often wondered whether the shame we as a nation have endured has imbedded that word in our culture. Unless we as a nation can get rid of all the feelings of guilt and victimhood we have cherished over lifetimes and really forgive ourselves and others, we cannot move forward to become the great nation we are meant to be.

Write Your Story:

- Do you have a story you want to write about your fear motivation and your luggage on the fear bus?
- Maybe you have motivated others through fear. Take time and write your story.

Summary

Forgiveness is a universal lesson that can lead to world peace. To forgive completely, we have to look at the luggage we carry around in our minds. Guilt can be likened to a virus, and it has extensions called shame and blame. That virus can ruin our lives if not dealt with properly. The world runs on fear motivation. It is our choice how we want to motivate ourselves and others.

The Biggest Lessons

Forgiving yourself and others can be very difficult, but it is our only way to inner peace. Forgiveness means we have to let go of shame, blame, and guilt. To be able to forgive yourself and others is the biggest act of self-love.

Word Reveal And The Power Of Words

In this chapter, I have written extensively about the words revealed in *Forgive*, namely Grief, Rife, Forge, Fire, Five, Or, Ogre. Forgiveness is another step on the fear bus to finding self-love and healing. I would like to mention again in the word Earth is Heart. To forgive heals — your heart and Mother Earth.

Rainbow Blessing

Thank you for the opportunities to forgive myself and others.

"One learns from books and example only that certain things can be done. Actual learning requires that you do those things."

— Frank Herbert

Chapter 8 — Forgetting: The Twin Of Forgiving

"To forget is to let go; to let go is to move on."
— Author Unknown

In the previous chapter, we saw shame and blame both refer back to guilt. Blaming is finding us or other people guilty. Shame is being the victim and feeling guilty about it. Once the mind takes guilt as the truth, we live according to those fear facts. In this chapter, we will look at the word forget.

Unveiling the word Forgive (Word Reveal)

Forget — Frog, Fret, Regret, Forge, Or, Ogre.

When I was working on these words, it was interesting to see many of the words hiding in forgive were also present in forget. That is why I call forgive and forget the twins.

Forgiving And Not Forgetting Keeps You On The Fear Bus

*"Do not let the shadows of your past darken the doorstep
of your future. Forgive and forget."*
— Author Unknown

Have you heard yourself or other people say, "I will forgive, but never forget"?

Forgive and forget are twin steps with the ability to free you from your fear chains. When I was working with forget, I said for a long time forgiveness was easier for me. I had to accept that things happened I could not forget. It was only when I learned about surrender that I could forget.

To understand the words hiding in forget, we will delve deeper into every word as we did with the words in forgive.

Frog — Shamans believe the frog is a power animal, a symbol of healing, cleansing, and rebirth. A frog is seen as an indication of transformation. Those who have worked through the process of forgiving and forgetting will tell you it is a life-changing transformation of healing, cleansing, and rebirth.

Fret — Other words for *fret* are worried, concerned, anxious, or losing sleep. Are you losing energy in such a way because you do not know how to work with forgive and forget?

Regret — Are you living with *regret*, which is a feeling of sadness, repentance, or disappointment over something you have failed to do? I like the saying, "Forgive and forget, not revenge and regret." It can only benefit us when working with forgiveness to remember the saying: Never regret your past. Accept it as the teacher it is. Our most significant opportunities will be found in times of greatest difficulty.

Forge — We hammer ourselves for years because we do not want to, or do not know how to, forgive and forget. Our ego, or the shadow, plays a big part in the process of forgiveness and forgetting. While anger, hatred, and playing the part of victim can give us energy for years, it is negative energy, and in the end, your health and relationships will suffer. No matter what your reason is for not forgetting, while you are holding on to that word, you are on the *fear bus*. Sometimes we do not know how to go on without the hatred, grief, and sadness we have carried for so long. Somehow, our feeling of importance is increased when we can tell the story of how awful our lives were.

Or — This word indicates our choice. We have to make the choice to change our lives. Nobody else can do it for us.

Ogre — I definitely had an aha moment when I realised this word is in forgive and *forget*. Unless we deal with both these words, we remain an ogre, and we will suffer the consequences by being in chains on our fear bus. There is a saying, "The first to apologise is the bravest. The first to forgive is the strongest. And the first to forget is the happiest."

How will you know you have really forgiven and forgotten? My answer: When you look at the situation or person and don't feel emotional poison anymore. Forgiveness is a lesson we keep on creating in our lives, maybe with different people, but causing the same feelings and triggering the same *emotion*, with the same results. (*Emotion* is energy going into motion or action.)

Write Your Story:

- How are you doing with forgetting?
- Write about some of the words you can associate with in the word forget.

Surrendering

One of the sayings I live by is, "Acknowledge, accept, surrender, and let go." During our journey on the *fear bus*, we have *faced* the *facts* and acknowledged that we had a lot of lies in our *belief systems*. We accepted and worked on the luggage of shame, blame, and guilt. We forgave ourselves and others. I often say in my courses, *To surrender means to yield*. The person who yields in a relationship is always the winner because he or she saves the relationship. Then the ego cannot play the shame, blame, and guilt game anymore. To yield on a road means you can avoid an accident or possible death.

Surrendering can also be to forget or discard what happened in our past. Don Miguel Ruiz says to surrender is to be happy under any circumstances. It is in forgetting and letting go that we can find ourselves. We have learnt during the process of transformation that we surrender to the fears that arise. Accept the old lies in your belief system, file them away, and open your arms to welcome the magnificent new life coming towards you from the future. (*Lies, file*, and *life* are all words revealed in *belief system*.)

I love to tell the story about the master who called his disciples to the edge of a cliff. He said to them, "Come closer." But they refused because they were afraid. He called them again, and they said, "We are afraid you will push us and we will die." He called them a third time. They came to the edge; he pushed them and they flew.

To break free from the chains of blame, shame, and guilt, we have to step over the edge into nothingness, let go of our past luggage, and "free fall" to experience the liberation and joy as we open our hearts and minds to a new way of thinking.

"Forgiveness and letting go are
steps on our road back to happiness."
— Tina Dayton

Remember, when you forgive, you heal, and when you let go, you grow.

Write Your Story:

• Have you dealt with surrender?

• Write a few lines about how you felt when working through this step.

Exercise — Putting It in the Pot

Please read through this exercise first before you do it. It can be a very emotional exercise for many people. If you need help with it, you are welcome to contact me.

In South Africa, a three-legged pot is associated with food where family and friends gather. Many years ago, as I stated earlier, when I started with my spiritual coaching, teenagers came to me with their problems, even suicidal tendencies. They were looking for an ear to listen to them. The only rule was they could not do anything drastic unless they had come back to me and the pot. The pot was our container, a safe place to put food in or, in this scenario, emotional issues. This was our container of forgiveness and forgetting. In forgive, there is the word fire, which is the "energy."

Take ten minutes to choose a person or situation you would like to forgive. Write a letter to the person (even if he or she has left the relationship, died, or you have no contact with the person any more). Say whatever you want to say — get it all out of your system. When you have finished, fold your letter and put it in your "pot"— the pot can be any place you choose.

I suggest you concentrate on one issue, giving it your full attention. Sometimes one major trauma influences our behaviour for the rest of our lives.

90

Doing the Exercise:

Close your eyes. Take a deep breath. Think of one thing or a person you fear or cannot get out of your system.

How do you feel? Can you taste it?

Can you associate a colour with the situation? Do you hear a sound?

Is there a smell you associate with it?

Keep breathing and know that you can experience strong emotions, but they are all in your mind and thoughts. The real situation is not happening to you at this moment. When you are ready, open your eyes and start to write your letter.

You can put your letter in an envelope and seal it when you are finished. Put it in your safe place — your pot. Take a few deep breaths and get up.

Go for a walk, or take a shower. Put on some uplifting music. Do something to celebrate the "mind meal" you have just made for your soul.

Write Your Story:

• You can use a separate page or write in your special book as you work through this exercise.

Bringing Twins Into Your Life Changes It Forever

> *"The end of old ways, beliefs, or situations occur so you can flow, align, and expand into greater awareness."*
> — Jasmine Safi

Transformation can be a scary process if we do not know how to work through it. You can give yourself a standing ovation for getting to this part of the book.

Knowing how to deal with the ego and the luggage on the *fear bus* will, hopefully, make it easier for you to enjoy your life's journey. I would like to leave you with a quote from Edward Wallis Hoch that my mother used many times to teach me not to be judgemental. "There is so much good in the worst of us, and so much bad in the best of us, that it hardly becomes any of us to talk about the rest of us."

Write Your Story:

- Did the last two chapters help you let go of things or people who have wronged you and kept you in chains?
- Write how you feel now after working through these last two chapters.

Summary

Understanding how to surrender is an important part of the process of forgetting. Putting our emotional baggage in the *pot* gives us the chance to look at our problems in an unemotional way and let go. Working with the twins — forgive and forget — can change your life for the better.

The Biggest Lessons

Forgetting does not mean you can forget the event. It means you feel no emotional charge when you see the cause of your pain or think about the painful situation.

Word Reveal And The Power Of Words

Forget — Frog, Fret, Regret, Forge, Or, Ogre. This is another step on your healing journey. I always find in my workshops after we have worked with *Forgive* and *Forget*, the energy in the group is much higher than before these exercises. I hope when you worked through these chapters you also felt a lightness of being.

Rainbow Blessing

I am grateful I can find happiness under all circumstances.

Chapter 9 — Having Fun

"Joy does not simply happen to us.
We have to choose joy and keep choosing it every day."
— Henri Nouwen

The twins, namely forgive and forget, we worked with in the last two chapters opened me up to learning about having fun. In Chapter 9, I would like to share with you this last word in my fear chain — fun — and our perceptions about it.

Note — we can have fun even if we are on the *fear bus*. In fact, we can become a *fun chaser*, trying to get away or forget at least for a few hours or a few days the emotional fear we are not aware of or do not know how to manage.

Synonyms for fun are: entertainment, excitement, diversion, distraction, good times, having a ball.

Fun becomes a *fear chain* word when it is rooted in running away from ourselves and our problems. The outside world is a great help in providing all kinds of fun, such as liquor, parties, entertainment places, and even social media — they are all there to enjoy. Participating in these types of fun, you have to ask yourself this one question, "Am I trying to fill a void or escape reality with my kind of fun?" If fun is your way to escape from your fears, you know it is not really fun.

Questioning Fun

Are you having fun?

The anonymous quote, "You never realise how boring your life is until someone asks what you like to do for fun", made me realise there are as many understandings of what is fun as there are people.

I realised I had no fun, or at least not the kind of fun other people thought of as fun, during one of my workshops. I agree with Noel Coward who says, "Work is much more fun than fun." I enjoyed my work, and by doing workshops on humour in the workplace, I thought I was having fun. I felt good about my kind of fun until I stopped to question what fun is for me. For me, fun was a long walk in nature or on the beach, dinner with a few friends, and reading books from one of my many book teachers. I did not think I should have more amusement in my life.

Listening to stories about wild parties or people gambling away thousands of dollars, and calling it fun, opened my eyes to the different ways we can chase after fun on the *fear bus*. Defining my kind of fun helped me to increase the way I have fun and make fun a part of my daily life. I now understand for me fun is to be happy in every moment. When I asked a very wise friend what she understood about fun, her answer was simple: "Many people think fun will bring them happiness or make them forget their troubles. Fun is something you do to relax and that you enjoy so much it makes you forget about everything, even time."

Although I was working on my last fear chain word, I was still learning about self-love, and fun is a big part of self-love. In the beginning, I had to focus *My Energy* on fun stuff for me. Starting my day with gratitude, doing an act of random kindness during the day, and ending my day with a blessing was for me a good start on the fun chain. In between, I did my work to the best of my ability, adding my kind of humour with much laughter and joy.

Write Your Story:

- Take a minute to define what fun is for you.
- Ask yourself whether your kind of fun is harming other people or yourself.
- Does your fun hurt animals?
- Is it ruining nature?
- Maybe your fun is your way of covering old wounds you are trying to forget.
- Is it really fun, or has it become an addiction, like drinking, working, or gambling too much? There are many fun things that can become dangerous addictions and keep us safely in our seats on the *fear bus*.

- When you have written down your answer, put it in your p*ot* or safe place with your letter, and leave it there until you feel you can safely look at your problem without the negative charge of emotion.
- Then burn your writings in your *pot*, or tear it up and throw it into the wind.
- Have some kind of a ceremony and let it go. Now you can go celebrate the start of your new life, hopefully having real fun.
- You can also use your book to write down how you feel after you have questioned your kind of fun and the value this exercise had for you.

Summary

Questioning what *fun* means in our lives and how much fun we have can open our eyes to whether we are really having fun or just running away from our fear.

The Biggest Lessons

Fun can have different meanings for people. If we are on the fear bus, it is good to question our way of having *fun* to establish whether it really is fun or whether we are trying to hide because we cannot face our fears or we do not want to forgive and forget.

Word Reveal And The Power Of Words

The only word I could get out of *fun* as a *fear-chain* word was *un-fun*. In the beginning of my *Rainbow Journey* when I wrote down the *fear words*, I wrote down the word *fun* because my friends were telling me I have no fun. Asking myself what fun means for me and understanding we can use fun as a form of escape from our fear-filled lives helped me to consciously live fun, *lightening* my life as a *Flighter*, feeling that it relaxed me to be *fit to fight* in the *right* way instead of getting angry at myself and others. Looking at my reactions as a *Frighter, Flighter,* and *Fighter* on the *fear bus*, I found this step hard to work with, but it was as rewarding as all the other steps on my *Rainbow Roadmap* to heal myself and learn self-love.

Rainbow Blessing

May we all find our truth about the fun we have, and may our kind of fun never involve hurting ourselves and others. Find the jolly Yellow Ray inside you and play with sunbeams for fun.

Part II

Love Motivation

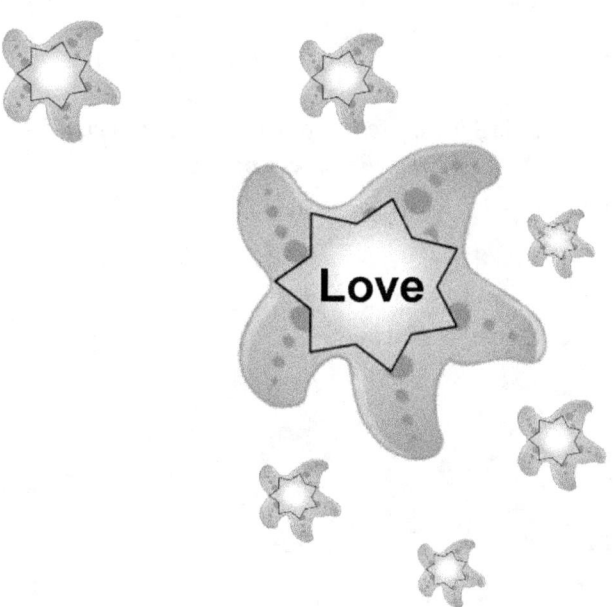

"There is no greater power in the universe than the power of love."

— Rhonda Byrne

Chapter 10 — Love: Making A Difference

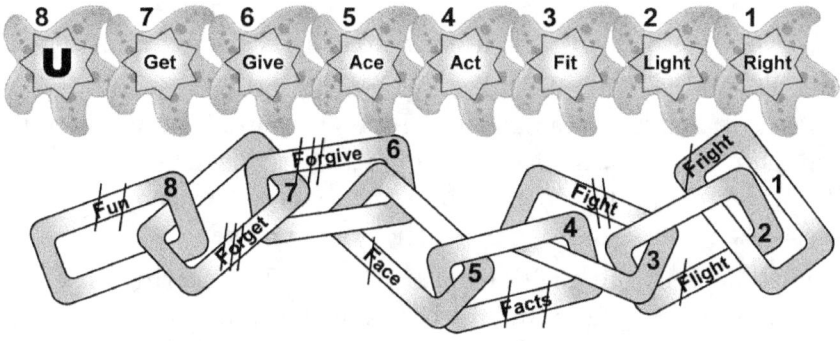

"We only hurt others, because we do not love ourselves.
Learning to truly love yourself
changes your relationship with everyone."
— Bryant McGill

In the first chapter of this book, I introduced you to fear and how we learn to react in fear due to our *domestication*. We called the reactions to fear the *fear chain*, and we used the *fear bus* as our vehicle on our *Rainbow Journey*. Introducing the *power of words* and changing our thoughts, feelings, words, and actions, we now understand *ME (My Energy)* and how we can start to manage our energy more effectively for our own health and wellbeing.

Every day, we make a difference at home, work, in our own and in other people's lives. The question we have to ask ourselves is: "Do I make a negative or positive difference?" In this chapter, where we start to delve into Love motivation, we *face the fact* that we are the vehicle, and we cannot walk away from the fear bus. However, we can change our thoughts, feelings, words, and actions so our vehicle becomes a *love bus*. I love the quote by Ward "Scarman" Foley: "We are not given a good life or a bad life. We are given a life. And it's up to us to make it good or bad."

The Miracle Of Love

"A miracle is a shift in perception from fear to love."
— Marianne Williamson

Have you ever been in a situation where you received the answer as if through a miracle?

In 1994, South Africa had a lot of fear as a nation. Nelson Mandela and the ANC (African National Congress) had just come into power. People were afraid for many different reasons. The saying that fear describes a state of mind, not an action, is very true.

I had been working with my *fear chain* while exploring life on the *fear bus*. I was trying to find the opposite of fear, but to no avail. One Sunday morning, I sat at my kitchen table and wrote down all the fear words. Having played with words and come to understand that answers can be in the word itself, I looked at my fear list. The next moment, a thought crossed my mind that I could take away the Fs in my fear words.

All the words made sense except in fight I kept the "f" and took away "g-h" to get fit, and in fun, I deleted "f and "n", leaving me with "u", which I read as "you", meaning myself. In forgive and forget, I deleted "for."

Fright	=	Right
Flight	=	Light
Fight	=	Fit
Facts	=	Acts
Face	=	Ace
Forgive	=	Give
Forget	=	Get
Fun	=	U

In the word fear is ear, which brought me to the word listening. Did you know during the development of our personal skills, we use our listening ability the most, speaking the second most, then reading comes third, and writing last. However, in school, we are taught to write the most, then to read, with speaking skills developed later. Very seldom are we taught how to listen. Is it any wonder some people find meditation and listening to their inner voice so difficult? Taking away the "f" in fear gave me the word ear. I associated the word ear with the word listen. Wondering to what or whom I am supposed to listen, the word heart came to mind. I saw the words hear and ear in heart. I wrote the sentence: "Listen to your heart." By associating heart with love, in that moment I knew the opposite of fear is love.

After months of trying to find the opposite part of my fear chain, the *roadmap* fell into place within minutes. What started as aspects of energy management and the meaning of words became in that moment my life's purpose. It also became the basis for the way I live my life on my *fear and love bus* while painting my world with rainbow colours. Following is the basic structure for the concept of my teachings namely – ME (My Energy) ROADMAP:

Fear Aspects:	Love Aspects:
Fright	Right
Flight	Light
Fight	Fit
Facts	Acts
Face	Ace
Forgive	Give
Forget	Get
Fun	U

Write Your Story:

- Have you ever had a moment of truth when you knew with clarity you had just experienced something greater than you could have imagined?

- If you have never experienced such bliss, write how it will feel if you find the answer to having a wonderful life in minutes.

Making A Difference In Life

"Never doubt that one person can make a difference."
— Ingrid Newkirk

At the beginning of this chapter, I said we all make a difference in life every day. The question we have to ask ourselves is: What kind of a difference?

Many of you probably know this story, but when I heard it the first time many years ago, it made such an impact on me that I decided to bring it into my book to remind me about the difference one person can make. Finding the opposite words to my *fear chain* and seeing one of the synonyms for an Ace (Chapter 15) is star, I knew why I love this story.

When we start to break the chains of fear, we all become stars or Star Throwers. In Part II, we learn how to change the *fear chain* to *love stars*.

The Star Thrower

An old man was walking on the beach early in the morning. He saw a young man picking up pebbles and throwing them into the sea. As he got closer, it turned out the man was not throwing pebbles into the sea, but picking up starfish that had been washed up on the beach as the tide came out.

Reaching the young man, he asked him what he was doing. The young man replied that he was picking up starfish and throwing them back into the sea because the sun was coming up and the tide going out. The starfish would die if he did not throw them back into the sea. The old guy then said to him there were miles of beach and thousands of starfish washed up on the beach. He had no chance of making a difference.

The young man bent down again, picked up a starfish, threw it back into the sea, and said: "It made a difference to that one."

Write Your Story:

- What kind of a difference are you making in your own life and the lives of others?
- Write a few lines on how you make a difference every day.

Learning To Change My Energy

Have you been in situations where you shared your knowledge but other people did not find it interesting or exciting?

I was exploring new paths on my journey in the newly painted love bus. I changed the yellow bus, which is all about finding your inner power and getting rid of fear, into a red bus. The red colour is associated with love, but it is also about manifesting your needs with ease as your higher energy frequency attracts new opportunities and people into your life, bringing you security and stability. Everything was new. I had to unlearn so much of my fear-based life that I found the following saying very appropriate: "You can't start the next chapter of your life if you keep rereading the last one."

I mentioned before I did not want to write a book and had many excuses when people told me to write. My biggest excuse was many wonderful teachers have already written books and given lectures all over the world, and they do it much better than me. One book that had a life-changing effect on me was *The Light Shall Set You Free* by Dr Norma Milanovich and Dr Shirley McCune. When I read their book, I was already exploring energy frequencies. They wrote: "Everything is energy and all energy moves and evolves in a circular way. At a microscopic level, we are nothing but a whirling mass of electrons and atoms, spinning rapidly. We are the sum total of our thoughts, feelings, words and actions." Back in 1998, reading this book made perfect sense to me because I had already experienced Albert Einstein's description that "Everything is energy and that is all there is to it. Match the frequency of the reality you want and you cannot help but get that reality. It can be no other way. This is not philosophy. This is physics."

My biggest challenge was to change my thoughts, feelings, words, and actions so my vehicle could change from a *fear* to a *love bus*.

Talking about love motivation in South Africa in 1994, especially in the business world, was just not done. Most men, managers, and business people, in general, got very uncomfortable. An office space was seen as a serious workplace where fear motivation was the norm. Organisations did not want to change; neither did they know how to become love-motivated companies. Even today, more than twenty years later, many companies are still operating on principles of fear motivation.

A manager at a company I worked with said to me, "I can understand what you say, that fear is an innovation killer, but fear motivation works to get the job done." I answered: "At what cost? In employee relations, productivity, sick leave, and high employee turnover?" He laughed and responded: "No comment."

Write Your Story:

- How difficult will it be for you to start to live love in your life, especially in your work environment?

- Write down a few ideas for how you can implement love.

Defining Love

What is Love?

One of my book teachers was Leo Buscaglia PhD (March 31, 1924 – June 12, 1998). Also known as "Dr. Love", Buscaglia was an American motivational speaker, professor in the Department of Special Education at the University of Southern California, and the author of Love. When his students asked him for the definition of love, his answer was very simple: "I cannot tell you — but follow me around and I'll show you." In those early years of learning about living love, Leo was an amazing teacher for me, and he touched the lives of many people all over the world.

I am aware that love can have as many definitions as there are people in this world. Living love for me means to learn to live in constant communication with my higher self on the frequency of gratitude, kindness, and happiness.

Changing my thoughts from negative to positive, I wrote small and big acts of kindness and love down in my diary. Here are some of my fondest memories of loving times. I remember from my childhood my father singing while he was getting ready for church. My mom's laughter while she was working in the house or making food is another loving childhood memory. I am convinced singing and laughing raised the vibrations of every person in our house.

I had cookies with milk many nights when I was a child and could not sleep. I slept with my parents in their room many a night if I was scared. I am so glad I grew up before self-soothing was a word. I know I would not have liked that.

My husband, our two children, and I can work together as a team, and some of my fondest memories are about the nights and days we worked together in our business, reducing the stress with good humour and much laughter.

My grandchildren throwing their arms around me for hugs and telling me they love me — those are memory jewels for me of learning, living, and loving on my rainbow journey.

Write Your Story:

- Have you got jewels in your memory jewel box?
- Can you name a few things big or small that make your heart sing?
- Write them down.

Believing In The Same Thing Again Is Totally Different

*"We can't solve problems by using the same kind of thinking
we used when we created them."*
— Albert Einstein

Have you questioned your belief system?

Who am I? That is a question I was faced with when I looked into the mirror one morning and a face stared back at me (Chapter 5). I could tell what I was doing and whom I was related to. I was like many other people, trying to juggle daily life and all its demands. I had no idea how to answer that question. I could say I am a perfectionist and I like to help people, but I felt a "lostness" in myself. It was impossible to describe the emptiness and sadness that looked back at me.

I mentioned before that my background was conservative. Like many Afrikaans-speaking, Christian households, I went to church and Sunday school, and believed with the faith of a child, but during my time of depression, I lost my faith in God. For many years, I would hear Spirit's voice, but I was a rebel. I said to God, "I am not going to do the work because it is too difficult." Although I went through a time when I felt godforsaken, and read widely about world religions, I tend to agree with Mahatma Gandhi who said, "God has no religion."

Religion is a manmade structure created by the followers of great prophets who lived and preached love. Fear motivation was brought into the structure by religious leaders to control their followers. Unfortunately, when fear walks in, love is often suppressed. I remember how shocked I was when I found many truths were left out of the Bible because those who compiled it knew certain truths would give the people too much power. The wonder is, in spite of inconsistencies, the Bible is still one of the most widely read books in the world.

I do not care what you call God. I do not see God as a person anymore, but God's energy can take many forms and has been given many names. I call God *Spirit of my Soul*. In moments of bitterness and despair, I have shouted at God, and like a naughty child, I have told God, "If there is a Jesus, He can find me." I was tired of looking for Him. I often say God can take our shouting.

God found me — standing naked under the shower. Many times, I have felt closest to *Spirit* under the shower. You cannot go anywhere under the shower; you have to listen to what is said. I often have discussions with God in the shower, and in the beginning, I thought it was my overactive mind thinking up all these stories. Then synchronicities started to happen. I would think of something under the shower and then hear a song or a sermon or open one of my spiritual books or cards and see the same words. Since I was hooked on words and their meanings, Spirit knew how to get my attention! If I was pondering or struggling with questions, books would come to me in profound ways — as gifts from people or by opening a book in a bookshop and reading the exact words for the answer I sought.

These words from the Bible, Isaiah 43:1, 4, and 5 (Good News Translation— GNT), often come to me:

> *I have called you by name — you are mine. You are precious to me, and because I love you, I am with you!*

One evening during our normal conversation under the shower, I told *Spirit* I will walk the road, but not one step without their protection and help. They answered: "You just turn up." I knew there was no turning back.

I believe every person has a spiritual calling, which is the real reason we come to earth. It's definitely not to go to school and study to get a job, fall in and out of love, make money, get sick, and then die. Everything that happens to us while we are here is to teach us about self-love and unconditional love. We live in a fear-filled world; we have to learn mostly through fear-based lessons. How do we know what good is if we have not seen evil or experienced fear? As I started to live love, I found I still believed in Christianity, but it was on a different energy frequency.

Write Your Story:

- Were you born into a religion you did not really feel comfortable with or believe in?
- Did you live your life without religion, and then had an experience that made you believe in a Higher Power?
- Maybe you are like me; you thought you believed in your religion, and then you went through a challenging situation and now you believe in that same religion, but from a different perspective.
- Relate your story.

Finding Many Truths Through Yoga

"Yoga means harmonising our words, our actions,
and our thoughts according to that sacred purpose.
The purpose is unselfish, humble service to God
and to all living beings. Love is the answer, a love that cannot
be disturbed by any circumstances
because it is the deepest essence."
— Anand Mehrotra

Have you found answers on your journey in places where you did not expect them?

In 1997, when I was still learning all the *facets* (remember the words face and facts from which I made facets) of unconditional love, I saw a small advertisement about yoga in the paper. With my very conservative background, which included the idea anything new or strange can be a sin, I still had many fears to overcome. I had read many books about spirituality and yoga and decided to find out for myself what yoga was about. I had only two yoga teachers in the years I did yoga. They were instrumental in me living my life with joy and happiness, and they both have my love. Now, many years later, I am teaching yoga myself in honour and gratitude for what my teachers have taught me. Yoga for me is not about doing a perfect yoga pose — it is a way of living my life.

Only when I started to live and study the science of Hatha yoga did I realise, although it has roots in the Hindu culture, it is not a religion. Millions of people all over the world, belonging to different religions and cultures, practice yoga. Patanjali, who is seen as the father of Hatha yoga, said: "Yoga is the practice of quieting the mind." In our modern world, where we get bombarded by so many stimuli from the outside world and our minds are constantly in overload, I am in favour of adding some kind of meditation or yoga practice to the school curriculum.

My yoga experience has brought me closer to my faith and to an understanding of my body, mind, and spirit. Yoga means to unite. The yogi teacher Anand Mehrotra said, "Yoga is a spiritual science, devised by rishis in India millennia ago for achieving personal communion with the Divine."

In my yoga journey, I asked myself who I am and why I am here. I believe we are here to learn about the *facets* of love through the different relationships we have, not only with ourselves and other people, but with animals, nature, and learning to see the Divine in everything. The ultimate is to experience an inner peace and happiness that cannot be disturbed by any outside circumstances because we acknowledge the infinite spark that is God within each of us.

The breath is God living in us — the energy we cannot survive without. Living with that awareness, we have to take care of our bodies because they are vehicles for God's breath. This was my answer to "Who am I?" It completely changed how I see myself. I have said I believe we all have a higher purpose. Through yoga, I learnt to harmonise my "thoughts, feelings, words, and actions" according to that sacred purpose. Love has a high frequency, and if you are tuned into that frequency, you have respect and compassion for all living beings.

Working with people who have awakened to their true potential and become the loving beings they are supposed to be is always an honour and brings me great joy.

In yoga, we say the realised and unrealised souls look the same, but inwardly, the unrealised person struggles with feelings of fear like shame, blame, and guilt. The realised soul has self-love and, therefore, also loves humanity.

I would like to tell a lovely story one of my teachers told us in class. It demonstrates beautifully that from the outside the person who is aware and the person who is not, look the same.

Two people are doing the dishes, but are they doing the same thing? One is thinking while doing the dishes: "It is not fair. I am also tired. Everybody else is sitting in front of the television." Their self-talk may take them deeper into anger and resentment and feeling like a victim. The other person is doing the dishes in a meditative state with gratitude for the food and is seeing God's grace in each plate. Before I went through my dark night of the soul, I believed in and spoke to God, who was living outside of me. Now I believe in and listen to God living inside me. Am I doing the same thing?

Write Your Story:

*   Have you found the Divine Spark in yourself?
*   Maybe you also found your divinity in a place you did not expect to find it.
*   Tell your story.

Summary

Receiving the *roadmap* for love took only a few minutes. Within those minutes, my life's purpose became the journey of love. I started to break the *chains of fear* and changed them into *stars of love*. Love is still a word very few in the business world understand. Living love for me meant learning to live in constant communication with my higher self on the frequency of gratitude, kindness, and giving freely. Yoga is so much more than doing physical exercises. For me, it is a way of living my life.

The Biggest Lessons

Everything is energy, and living with the energy of love brings happiness.

Experiencing bliss while we go through our daily challenges is possible only through a peaceful mind.

Rainbow Blessing

May your thoughts be filled with light. May your words be filled with kindness. May your hearts rejoice in Love.

Chapter 11 — Choosing Right Over Fright

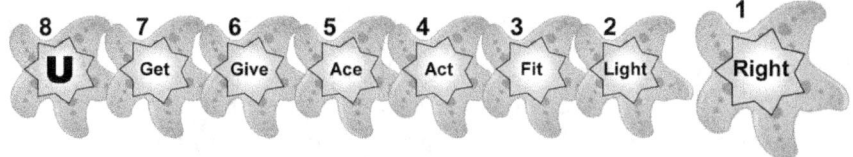

*"There is no right or wrong behaviour.
The only meaningful choice is between fear and love."*
— Gerald Jampolsky

Chapter 10 started the journey on the *love bus*. In this chapter, the chain word *fright* becomes the star word *right*. In the previous chapter, I told the story of the Star Thrower. Breaking away from "freezing" in the fright reaction to fear, we release the *fear chain* as we become "Star Throwers", saving our own and other peoples' lives.

Abraham Maslow said, "What is necessary to change a person is to change his awareness of himself." Knowing my reaction when in fear, namely as a *Frighter*, *Flighter*, and *Fighter*, helped me find the right key to unlock my potential. Learning to live love and working with the word *right*, I had to figure out what I had to do right in my life.

Deepak Chopra said, "To make the *right* choices in life you have to get in touch with your soul."

Making The Right Choices For Me

I made the following list for myself about the right choices:

- Learn the right breathing techniques and meditation so I can breathe next time I am in a stressful situation.

- Learn to act immediately instead of postponing or procrastinating.

- Watch less news and listen to more uplifting programmes especially before going to bed at night.

- Read my correspondence an hour later in the mornings instead of starting my day with a text or phone call.

- Take loving care of my body with healthy food and exercise and doing fun things for me to nurture self-love.
- Have my internal GPS on about my thoughts, feelings, and words.

Learning to take the *right* action in situations where I freeze led me to read books like *The Four Agreements* and *Beyond Fear* by Don Miguel Ruiz, who is one of the book teachers who inspired and influenced my love journey.

Write Your Story:

- If you are a *Frighter*, list some positive actions you can take to prevent yourself from *freezing* out of fear.

Righting Wrongs

"And you?
When will you begin the long journey into yourself?"
— Rumi

How many times have you heard or said, "No, don't do that. It is wrong." A good family friend with a wonderful sense of humour says he was thirteen before he realised his name was not *Don't* as he felt it was the only word he heard as a child.

Looking at the word *fright* in the fear chain and changing it to *right* — by dropping the "F"— brought me to the question of right and wrong. I have accepted we live in a world of duality and most people learn through fear. Instead of choosing *fright*, you can start to choose *right*. I used the *pot* as my term of reference; I started to see my body and mind as the *pot*. It was easy for me to come up with examples of right: Eat the right food, do the right exercise, listen to good music, or choose television programmes with care. What I put into my mind became as important as what I put into my body.

One of the first steps in my teachings to help people to change their thoughts from fear to love is to say "Stop" when they catch themselves thinking or saying words with a low vibration.

Many clients come to me complaining about their close relationships. I once had a client complaining about her husband. When I told her she should keep in mind that behind every man is a woman — his mother — she burst out laughing and said that explains it all. Although it lightened the mood, she quickly saw the relevance of my remark. She said she had two sons she would start to teach to treat women with respect and consideration, which were the two problems she had with her husband. Once we realise we attract on the outside what we have to learn to overcome in ourselves, it makes life easier for us. She went home and started to treat her husband with respect and more consideration and gratitude for what he was doing for them, and the next time I saw her, she excitedly told me that without any effort from her side, he changed his behaviour toward her.

My client also reported that as she changed and became more respectful and considerate towards her mother-in-law, she saw what a loving and wonderful person the mother really was, so their relationship also turned to love instead of fear reactions like blame and guilt.

Working with a male client whose first words to me were: "I am a God-fearing man" was a lesson for me in how we can heal many relationships when we understand that our words can be swords hurting people we love. After the second session, in which we worked with the fear-chain reactions and how we see God and he was introduced to the love stars, he looked at me and said, "I am not a God-fearing man. Those were fear motivated words. I am a God-loving man."

When he first came to see me, he liked to tell me derogatory jokes about women, but as he started to change from fear and shameful behaviour to living love and forgiving himself and others, he realised those jokes were low frequency and not sacred words with love. As his attitude changed, he reported to me how much his relationship with his mother, wife, and daughters changed, and for the first time, he felt he could really say he was living for God's honour and glory because his relationships mirrored so much love back to him.

Awareness means to look at the world with new eyes and know you can make choices. I believe living in a world of duality is good for us. Learning to say "no" teaches us about boundaries and when to say "yes." We cannot define happiness without experiencing what it is to be unhappy.

During one of my Granny sermons, I told my own grandchildren that tearing apart flowers in bloom without any reverence for the flower or plant is like killing a little animal or a baby. No child will hurt the earth and her inhabitants willingly if they know plants and animals can feel fear. Many tests have shown that plants respond to love. Gandhi said, "The greatness of a nation and its moral progress can be judged by the way its animals are treated." I would like to add "by the way all life on Earth is treated."

I love the story of the teacher who wrote the nine times table on the blackboard and started with 1 x 9 = 7. She finished the whole table without any more mistakes. The children were laughing and telling her she had made a mistake. She said, "I did that on purpose. You saw the one mistake, but you did not mention I had all the other answers correct."

Intolerance and judgmental behaviour belong to the *fear bus*. Creating a culture of tolerance and acceptance is another step towards *righting wrongs*. As human Masters of this Earth, it is our responsibility to be alert and show the generations to come how to take care of their legacy.

In Chapter 2, I wrote about the resistance against religion due to so many *lies* we have been fed. Maybe it is time to look at religion and spirituality from a different frequency, and instead of speaking about it as two different poles, see it as it was meant to be — the church and religion as the body or vehicle for our spiritual development and a safe place to connect with our *Godness* where children learn about respect and self-love for their bodies, for other people, and for every living thing on earth as their birth right. In that way, they can make better choices when they grow up living their truths. I would like to end this story with a quote from the Buddha: "Just as a candle cannot burn without fire, men cannot live without a spiritual life."

Write Your Story:

- Write down what you would like to change in your life to right the wrongs you are doing.
- Maybe you would like to learn to eat healthy food, drop some of your favourite television programmes, or quit playing games loaded with bad language and violence.

Choosing One Master

> *"Sometimes you face difficulties not because you're doing
> something wrong, but because you're doing something right."*
> — Joel Osteen

Have you ever had the experience of thinking about something and then getting the answer through a sentence in a book or a song you heard?

Working through my fear reactions, I kept getting words from the Bible: "You cannot serve two masters." I know the verse very well. In 1 Kings 18:21 and 2 Kings 17:41, I found my answer.

1 Kings 18:21 says: "Elijah came near to all the people and said, 'How long will you hesitate between two opinions? If the Lord is God, follow Him; but if Baal, follow him.' But the people did not answer him a word." 2 Kings 17:41: "So while these nations feared the LORD, they also served their idols; their children likewise and their grandchildren, as their fathers did, so they do to this day."

I asked myself what was the truth for me in these verses? I came to the conclusion in spite of religion and spirituality and all our modern in-between beliefs, many people still keep choosing between right and wrong, good and evil, or rather the big word sin. I prefer to use the word evil, for in it is the word live. I have seen people concentrate so much on what is sinful or evil that they do not live their lives.

The Bible also says not to judge, but that is one of the passages we choose to ignore. In our everyday lives, we judge ourselves and others on the smallest of things. I am always shocked into total silence, which is a rare experience for me, when I hear people concentrating or having a "lock-on" about certain words and missing the beauty of the story because they listen or read with their minds instead of their hearts.

Realising what I was doing myself helped me choose. I was born into the Christian belief system, and after my journey through the desert, I am still a Christian. I find it difficult to understand why Christians still choose to live in fear and concentrate on sin. We proclaim the Christ came to Earth to live as a man and died a horrible death so people could wake up and love one another. Two masters — Live or Evil. Are we still chasing after a master that does not bring us the love, happiness, and peace we all desire?

I made my choice to live. I have said before in the word believe there is lie and live. Eldon Tanner said it so aptly:

> One of God's greatest gifts to man is freedom of choice. At an early period in the journey through life, man finds himself at a crossroad where he must choose one of two great highways — the right, leading to progress and happiness; and the wrong, leading to retardation and sorrow. There exists this eternal law that each human soul, through the choices he makes, will shape his own destiny. Our success or failure, peace or discontent, happiness or misery, depend on the choices we make each day.

While getting through my depression, I used the phrase "moment by moment." I still live moment by moment, making it the best, most loving moment I can have. Life happens, but instead of getting stuck in a moment that was challenging, I let it go with the attitude of surrendering, which for me is being happy in all circumstances.

It was a difficult lesson for me to stop being a *worrier* about what can go wrong and to become a *warrior* at getting excited about what can go right. It helped me to understand worrying is mostly the ego looking for attention, and I am not running a race against my shadow anymore.

Write Your Story:

- What are you choosing that makes it easier for you to live instead of judging others and finding evil everywhere in this world?
- Write your story about your choice.

Summary

Making the right choices is the start of living love. Understanding we live in a world that has been motivated by fear for thousands of years and that many of our beliefs are based on fear helped me break free and choose the master called love.

The Biggest Lessons

Make a list of the things you want to change from *fright* behaviour to *right* behaviour, on the physical, emotional, and mental levels.

Word Reveal And The Power Of Words

The word reveal in *fright* is *right*. Words revealed in *evil* are *live* and *lie*. In Chapter 5, I discussed the words revealed in *belief system*. Here are some words revealed in *believe* — *lie, live, evil, vile, veil*. As you can see, many words have the *fear* and *love* meanings in the same word. Once we know about *fear and love motivation*, it is our choice how we want to make a difference.

Rainbow Blessing

Thank you for the clarity to make the right choices.

"Beauty is not in the face; beauty is a light in the heart."
— Kahlil Gibran

Chapter 12 — Finding Light Instead Of Flight

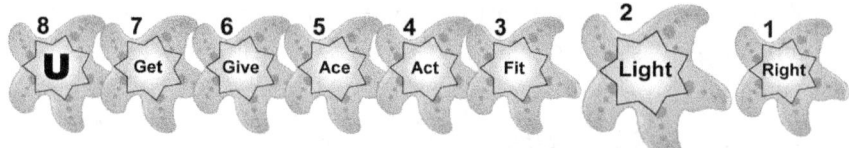

"Don't you know yet? It is your light that lights the world."
— Rumi

In Chapters 10 and 11, we looked at changing our reaction from fear to love and from fright to right. In Chapter 12, the flight reaction to fear turns to light.

Take away the "F" in Flight and you have the next love star word on the *love bus* as a Star Thrower and a champion, which is light. If you start to do the right things — eat right, get proper exercise for your body and personality, start feeding your mind with good thoughts, and becoming aware of what you are doing with your energy daily — life becomes lighter. Do not be surprised if you lose some body weight in this process. If we start to move away from fear, we feel so much lighter.

I have Jasmine Safi's wonderful deck of Rainbow Cards. On the Light Frequencies card are these words: "The universe responds to your vibrational frequency. Tune your frequency into love."

People who live happy, joyful lives have a lightness of being about them that attracts like-minded, positive people. If you stick to your new way of living in love rather than fear, your outer surroundings will also change. There are many stories about people who changed their whole way of living by changing their negative and fear-motivated thoughts and feelings into uplifting thoughts, feelings, words, and actions. Do not think it will be an easy road in the beginning. When I was still in primary school, a teacher told us when learning new "things", we have to repeat it a few times to form a pathway in our brain. Using the pathway is like planting little trees along that path. Since then, I have a picture

119

in my mind that the more we use a specific pathway in the brain, the better we get at doing something and planting a forest in our minds. The opposite is also true that to unlearn a negative pattern, we have to take out that whole forest in our mind. To change and remove a whole forest of negativity in your mind is one of the most difficult, but also most rewarding, steps to change your *flight* reaction to *fear* into a *love star* of *light*.

Lightning Up The Skies

"You have to find what sparks a light in you so that you in your own way can illuminate the world."
— Oprah Winfrey

While growing up in the Northern Cape, in South Africa, my favourite time of day was the morning while I was waiting for the school bus. I would close my eyes and peep through my eyelashes at the rising sun. If I did it in the right way, I could see the sun through a prism of rainbow colours. I would have missed the bus many times while doing this if my mom had not warned me to stop playing.

At sunset, watching the sun going down behind the hills in the west in all its splendour and knowing that somewhere in the world it was sunrise, always brought me a feeling of safety. Doe Zantamata says: "Choose to see the world through grateful eyes. It will never look the same again." As a ten-year-old child, I did not think a lot about gratitude, but the sun was a constant source of wonderment.

The Northern Cape is an area with frequent thunderstorms. Listening to the thunder, watching the lightning play, and smelling the rain always filled me with awe. Running from one window to another after a thunderstorm in search of a rainbow was always a source of joy for me. That is not to say I did not have a holy respect for the power of the lightning. Due to where we were on the hill, we had a lightning conductor on the highest point of our house. My parents often told us the story of how the lightning once hit the house when the previous owner still lived there, and how the people living in the house were all saved, because they were asleep on their wooden beds. The lightning conductor was only put up when my father bought the farm.

Why, you may ask, am I writing about the weather? The rainbow colours I could see through my lashes and the sunsets in all those beautiful shades and tints of red, pink, orange, and yellow started a journey that would become my life purpose. Little did I know while I was drinking in the colours of the sun and searching for the rainbow after a storm at the age of ten, how big a role the rainbow colours would play in my future.

Write Your Story:

- Relate your experiences about the beauty and influence nature had on you as a child.

Being A Pleaser With Ease

Have you realised as you let go of old habits that do not serve you anymore, you are more at ease with yourself and others? See the Word Reveal and the Power of Words at the end of this chapter.

Facing the facts and changing my thoughts made me realise how powerful my inner light could be. As I learnt more and more about vibrations and frequencies, I experienced working with light vibrations and positivity makes life so much easier. I was still a pleaser. I like to do things for people. After I worked through forgiveness and let go of the shame, blame, and guilt, I could please myself and others with ease. By changing my attitude about serving others and starting to do it with gratitude and humility, without expecting anything back, I was not taken for granted anymore. In fact, people were grateful for every little thing I did for them. I was still on the bus, but it had become the *love bus*. My vehicle of light was travelling on new roads, and I experienced much joy weaving my light into my own life and the lives of others.

Write Your Story:

- Name a flight reaction you had to fear (e.g. a poisonous pleaser) and describe how you changed your attitude to see the same characteristic now as a positive.

Finding Your Inner Light

Have you found the truth about your inner light and how you can share it with the world?

Jasmine Safi says on her Rainbow Card about Resonant Truth: "Being in resonance with your soul brings all things to light."

I believe we come to Earth carrying the light of God within us. I think it is inherent in many people to want to make the world a better place. A good beginning is healing ourselves first before we can heal the world or any other person. Due to the duality we experience on earth, we sometimes forget who we really are. The struggles of life and the fear and negativity we all go through, before we can acknowledge the light inside us, can keep us from living our real magnificence. The further apart from our God purpose we are, the more afraid, angry, or lonely we feel.

Since childhood, I will become physically sick when I see people treat animals or plants without respect. I can literally feel the animal or plant's fear and pain. I have cried at a tree stump because it was cut down without any love or respect. During one of my meditations, when I asked Spirit about my purpose, the answer was: "You are my *cell.*"

I had written a story for my grandchildren about a character named *Cell* coming to earth, so I immediately understood this answer. When I asked what cell stands for, the answer was: "Cosmic Essence Living Love." That made total sense to me! I like the idea that we are all cells, and as the cells light up, the earth will light up. With the recent earthquake in New Zealand, I said the earth is shaking to wake us up.

Write Your Story:

• Write about your journey as a *Flighter* and how you found your inner *light.*

Summary

Playing with the magnificent light of the sun and rainbows from an early age was a preamble to spreading my *light* and love in the world.

Working through our fear, we often find we still have the same characteristics but our attitude towards them has changed.

Working with your inner light does not mean you have to be an energy worker or a healer. Opening your heart and standing up for yourself instead of hiding behind others can let your light shine.

The Biggest Lessons

Life becomes lighter when we find our inner *light* and consciously use it to spread love throughout the world.

Word Reveal And The Power Of Words

Here are some words revealed in *pleaser*: asleep, ease, seal, real, release, please, see, reap, ear, leap, and peel. The power of the words can be: When we awake from being *asleep* and *release* emotional poison, we *please* with *ease* and *reap real pleasure*.

Rainbow Blessing

Thank you that our inner light is embracing the world with love.

"The first and best victory is to conquer self."
— Plato

Chapter 13 — Getting Fit To Fight The Right Way

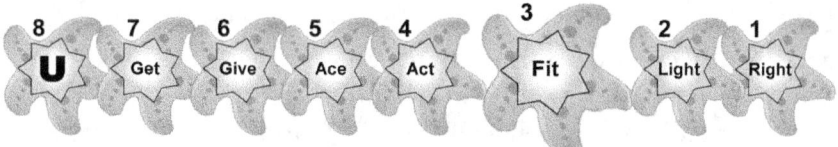

"Don't take anything personally.
Nothing others do is because of you."
— Don Miguel Ruiz

The love bus had a new reason for its journey through life, and as more and more light-minded people (pardon the slip of my tongue — it should be like-minded) joined me on the bus, our passion for a life lived in the *light* of love ignited the fire to become *fit* for the trip as *star throwers* or *champions*. In Chapter 4, we saw we can fight out of fear and use blame and shame as our weapons. In this chapter of our love journey, we will explore getting *fit* to fight in the loving way, serving humanity with glory and honour, starting to work on our own *fitness* first.

In *Fight*, we take away the G and the H and we get *fit*. As you grow into your new life, your mind and body become fit. Keep in mind when working with the examples on *Frighters, Flighters,* and *Fighters,* you established which aspects of fear you chose. You will always react in that way when you are in a stressful situation — we've worked on accepting yourself as you are, "facing the facts about you." The *fighters* in life are usually the leaders. Good news for the *fighters.* You can learn to become *fit* by living love and use your energy to create a world of peace, love, and abundance, instead of reacting or fighting from a fear-based belief system.

Becoming Fit To Fight In The Right Way

"The fearful seek to serve themselves by mastering the world, while the fearless seek to serve the world by mastering themselves."
— Eric Micha'el Leventhal

125

Do you know what is the right way for you to fight?

I said earlier I grew up in a family of strong personalities and *fighters*.

It is important to remember fighters are people who will stand up for others and not give up easily. It was only much later I realised fighters are sometimes like those described in the above quote. They seek to serve themselves by mastering the world. Unfortunately, if we look at many politicians and governments all over the world, the above statement seems to be true. The fear parasite is everywhere. An original idea can be pure and created with the best of intentions, but if the shadow part or ego comes into play, and people start to compete for power, they usually end up doing exactly the opposite of what the original idea was.

It still happens that shame, blame, and guilt are aimed at the person whom they think wronged them. By working with the process of forgiveness and changing ourselves, the dynamics in the relationship will change. While we are working through the situation or challenge, we cannot help our partners, children, or the people teaching us the lesson. Sometimes we have to let go of people to soar to a higher level of energy. In mastering ourselves, we can really serve others with humility and love.

I often have clients tell me after their first session they want other family members to come to me too. My reaction is always to have them ask the family member to contact me or come for a complimentary session to see what I do, and then the person can decide for him — or herself. We should never expect the therapy benefitting one person should be the therapy or the way to heal the other person in a relationship.

Write Your Story:

- Where are you on the *love bus*? Are you still *fighting* to make your mark in the world, or are you working through the fear to master yourself and be a leader who is strong enough to lead people because you know your inner power?

Fighting Fit

> *"Fitness means it is your responsibility to be the best*
> *and to take accountability for your deeds.*
> *Accountability breeds response-ability."*
> — Stephen R. Covey

What kind of fitness programme do you follow to become mentally and emotionally fit?

Many people do some kind of exercise for their physical bodies. For me, starting out to become *fit* on a mental and emotional level was difficult. In a world where we are mostly motivated through fear, to live love is often seen as weakness or indecision.

To become fit for a fulfilling joyful life, lived in love and abundance on all levels, we practice becoming fit in the right way. If you are a boxer, at some stage, you must go into a boxing ring. You cannot always just run long distance or jump rope. Knowing who you are makes it easier. The *Frighters, Flighters,* and *Fighters* all can find the right way for themselves. The word *right* is in all three of those fear-based words. The words *fit* and *fire* are also in all three words, showing us if we let go of our fear reactions and become *fit* in the *right* way to live love, we will ignite our inner *fire*, which is our true self. When I started to work on mastering myself many years ago, I made the same mistake many people do. I wanted my immediate family, and even friends, to share my journey and experience the exhilarating feeling of changing yourself.

I lost a few friends and most of my family had started praying for me before I realised to journey on the *fear* or the *love bus* is a choice, and even though you want it for those you love, they have to ride on their buses in their own way and in their own time. It was interesting to see as I changed, those around me changed without any help from me. One of my favourite sayings is "We rub off on people." The question is: Do I rub off fear or love? Starting to live love and looking at the world through grateful eyes rubbed off, and it was so much more rewarding for me to see how everyone in my family got onto the *love bus* in his or her own unique way.

My children, Brian and Anri, were both introduced to the Investment in Excellence training programme when they were still young. Growing up in a house where the word excellence was used a lot influenced them in different ways.

Recently, one of Brian's friends complained he had gained weight, so he asked Brian what he did to keep fit. Brian replied he did twenty push-ups and twenty sit-ups every night, which takes about five minutes. When the friend laughed and said that won't be enough for him to lose weight, my son said, "I do the exercises seven days a week, which amounts to 140 push-ups and 140 sit-ups a week. Doing a little each day allows me to do more than the person not doing any at all."

Looking back at how I shouted at God to get my anger out, and how I am talking to Spirit now when I have to work through anger, makes me realise my way of working towards mastery would not have worked for anyone else in my family. The beauty of it all is they are all having a wonderful trip and have found their own special ways of getting fit.

Write Your Story:

- What are you doing to get fit emotionally and mentally?
- Have you taken responsibility and accountability for your own life, meaning you are responsible for how you act, choosing between fear and love reactions?

  In many situations, we share responsibility with other people. We can all take responsibility to build a world of peace instead of war and destruction. Accountability means only you are answerable for your actions. Being accountable, you quickly get *fit* to *fight* in the *right* way because you have left shame, blame, and guilt on the fear bus.

- Write down what you plan to do, or are doing already, to be a *love warrior*.

Living Excellence Instead Of Competing

> *"Ultimate excellence lies not in winning every battle,*
> *but in defeating the enemy without ever fighting."*
> — Sun Tzu

How do you feel about excellence and competition?

Anri is a free-flowing kind of personality who puts visualization to work for her. One of her favourite sayings is "Work smarter, not harder." She started working for a big cellphone company in South Africa when she was twenty. Soon after she started working for it, she heard the company would give a car to the person who had won the title "best salesperson" three years in a row. I always told her when we went shopping in our local mall that I was invisible, because all her clients greeted her with so much enthusiasm and affection. After three years, she won the car. Her answer when asked how she did it: "All I visualised when I thought about the car was seeing my hands on the steering wheel and getting the smell of a new car."

In Chapter 4, I talked about competition and how the words "competing against" can cause many people to react with fear. Although I am a fighter and have competed in many ways, I prefer to talk about living excellence. Excellence came into my life when my husband, Weldon, received training at the Bristol Excellence Quality Centre in 1991. He was also trained as a facilitator for the Malcolm Baldrige Excellence Model and the European Excellence Model. Back then, I was the secretary for the South African National Association of Suggestion Systems (SANASS). Seeing recognition programmes in action, I had first-hand knowledge of how positive recognition can ignite excellence in people and companies.

Weldon has been and still is a role model to many people of someone living the culture of excellence. I admire his sense of pride, and I agree pride stands for Personal Responsibility In Delivering Excellence. One of his own quotes is: "Excellence is the result of going beyond what is practical, expected, and possible."

Due to Weldon's background and knowledge of Excellence Models, he co-developed the South African Excellence Model and was instrumental in many sectorial adaptations of it for the South African market. Excellence became our main focus when we bought the South African Excellence Model and Training Material Intellectual Property. We also changed our company name from Ideas Management Southern Africa to the Centre for Excellence. About 70 percent of all excellence model-related training in South Africa was done through our company. At that stage, our children, Brian and Anri, had both joined us as partners in our family business.

One of our most enriching and successful experiences happened during this time working together. We were contacted by Gert Wiese, the Officer Commanding of a Security Squadron in the South African Air Force. The Chief of the Air Force visited his unit and suggested he attend an excellence training course.

In Air Force culture, pilots were "top of the hierarchical ladder", and the security guards were not even "on the ladder"! After attending an excellence training course Weldon and Brian facilitated, Gert took the information, and brimming with initiative and energy, he went back to train the people in his unit. He applied the Excellence Model principles, not only at work, but also in practical ways outside of work igniting people in the community with the passion to come up with all kinds of ideas to make life easier for the less fortunate.

Gert embodied Ralph Marston's quote: "Excellence is not a skill. It is an attitude." Gert's capacity to take the people in his unit with him paid off when they won the South African Air Force Excellence Award. One day, a general, who visited the unit and wanted to see for himself how much excellence was practiced throughout the unit, asked the security guard at the gate, "Tell me what you know about Excellence?" The guard replied, "General, you will have to get out of the car." The general complied with his request, and then with a stick, the guard drew the Excellence Model in the sand and explained what all the blocks meant. I wonder what the general thought. Very few of the "top structure" would have been able to draw the model and name all eleven Excellence Criteria.

Excellence Model Sand Drawing

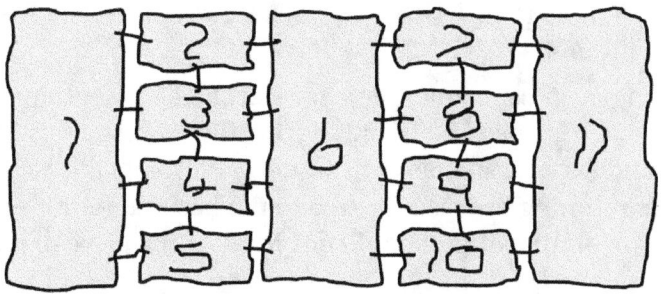

11 Criterion Parts of Excellence Model

1. Leadership 2. Policy & Strategy 3. Customer & Stakeholder Focus 4. People Management 5. Resources & Information Management 6. Processes 7. Social Responsibility 8. Customer & Stakeholder Satisfaction 9. People Satisfaction 10. Supplier & Partnership Performance 11. Organisation Results

We were very excited as a company to see how one person was making a difference not only in his own life, but, through his example, building his unit into a place where people had self-confidence and pride in living a culture of Excellence. When the unit started out, there were no proper offices. There was one building on the base in a dilapidated state. Money was not available for renovations, and not being an elite unit, it was left up to the unit members to fix the place. They worked weekends, assisted by their families, to restore the place. In Gert's office, the ceiling was so bad it could not be fixed.

One morning while Gert was in his office, he heard someone cutting down trees outside his office. He walked outside and stopped the felling of the trees, went back into his office and measured the distance between the floor and the ceiling. After he gave the tree cutters the measurements, they cut the tree to the exact length. The wood was varnished and put in his office to support the ceiling, and a parachute was used to cover the whole ceiling.

Weldon and I visited him in his office. He was bursting with excitement and creative ideas, and he was full of praise about how the Excellence Model had changed his life. We were all inspired by him and the amazing avalanche of positivity he had caused throughout his unit. Joel Osteen said: "When you have a spirit of excellence, you do the right thing not because somebody is watching or making you do it; you do it because it's the right thing to do." That was indeed true of Gert and the unsung heroes in his unit.

Shocking news came unexpectedly. Gert had a brain tumour. Brian and Gert had become good friends during the process of his excellence journey, and we were all hoping he would get through this very difficult time. The morning he was admitted to the hospital for his operation, he drew the outline of the Excellence Model on a piece of paper. He told his wife that when he regained consciousness, she could give him the paper, and if he wrote down the eleven criteria in the right blocks, she would know he was going to make a full recovery.

Unfortunately before the doctors could operate on him, he passed away due to complications. Brian was asked to deliver a tribute at his funeral, which was held in a military base hall. The hall was filled and people even stood outside to pay their last respects to a man who had been an unknown soldier a few months earlier and who did so much to build a culture of excellence people could live by. Brian concluded his tribute with these words: "You have been a 'Paragon' to us all — an extreme example of Excellence."

The unit continued to apply the principles of excellence to become the only government department ever to be awarded the prestigious South African Excellence Foundation Award. In honour of Gert, his wife was asked to receive the award on behalf of the whole unit. Gert passed away in 2004, but we still hold his memory close to our hearts. The legacy of Gert Wiese and how he inspired and ignited the flame of excellence in many people can be summarised with the words of Brad Lomernick, who said, "Chase after a level of excellence that will stretch you and astonish others." Indeed, Gert Wiese and his people did exactly that.

Write Your Story:

- Do you know someone who raised the bar of excellence to a higher level?
- Or maybe you raised it yourself?
- Write about your personal journey developing an attitude of excellence.

Outgrowing Our Cells

People think excellence is a word to use in the business world. Are you one of them?

Excellence is doing everyday tasks with awareness and passion in such a way they become your masterpiece. That way, every moment of every day you outgrow your own cells.

I once wrote a story for my grandchildren about Cell who came to Earth on the Rainbow Train. It tells the story of a soul that is going to be born to learn about love. Working with excellence, I decided to go with the description that "ex" is a prefix meaning "out of." Excellence, therefore, means literally outgrowing your own cells. Since we constantly renew our body's cells, I liked the idea that as we learn innovative ways to live love, we outgrow our old habits.

There is a saying, "If you want peace of mind, stop fighting with your thoughts." I practiced excellence by becoming aware of my thoughts while working around the house or garden.

Working from the viewpoint everything is energy, I am always aware of my thoughts while preparing food or ironing clothes. I am a firm believer that negative or positive feelings *rub off* onto my food or my family's clothes.

One morning while Weldon was in church, I made his favourite food, and while preparing the food, I listened to wonderful music from Andre Rieu. I was telling the food I love it and thanking it for feeding our cells with light and love. During the meal, Weldon said the food was really delicious. I reminded him it was his favourite dish, but he said it was extra special that day. It was then I realised we affect everything around us with our thoughts, feelings, words, and actions — and not only people, animals, or plants. Our influence on all matter around us is made clear in the books of Dr Maseru Emoto, in Linda Goodman's *Star Signs*, and in the works of many others who wrote extensively on this subject.

Alastair Arnott said: "Fighting against is easy. Fighting for requires wisdom, courage, and vulnerability." Remember we can all get into circumstances where we temporarily freeze. Within the word *Frighter* hides the *fighter* and also the one who knows what is *right*. Do not be scared to step out of your fear and act to do the right thing. If the

Flighters open up to their inner *light,* they will do *right,* and then when they take *flight,* they will soar high. *Fighters,* you do not have to fight because *fright* is hiding inside. Acknowledge your fear and also the *fire* in you. Do not *fight* wars that destroy lives, for you will not fulfil your (our) purpose. *Get fit* to fight *right* and save the world.

Write Your Story:

- Have you outgrown (ex-celled) your old life?
- Take a look at your own story.
- Then write down how far you have come since you began the *fear-* and *love bus* journey with me.

Summary

Fighters can learn to become fit to fight in the right way. This means finding your inner power to live love and create peace and abundance instead of fear, war, and poverty.

All change starts on the inside and requires mastering ourselves first instead of trying to change the world. It is good to have your own programme or plan for how you are going to get fit mentally and emotionally. An attitude of excellence is a good beginning.

Every thought, feeling, word, and action has an influence on the environment and people around us. To realise the smallest action can have a major influence makes it worthwhile to become *fit* to *fight* in the *right* way.

The Biggest Lessons

Work out a personal plan to become fit emotionally and mentally.

Word Reveal And The Power Of Words

In the words *Frighters, Flighters,* and *Fighters* are fright, fight, right, fit, and fire. Once again, we see that how we use words can be fear and love motivating. Letting go of our fear reactions, we become *fit* to *fight* in the *right* way to live love, to ignite our inner *fire,* and also to help others to ignite their fires instead of killing those fires with our fear motivation.

Rainbow Blessing

Blessings to all people who ex-cell every day without ever getting recognition. May their perseverance inspire others.

"One of the greatest discoveries a man makes, one of his great surprises, is to find he can do what he was afraid he couldn't do."

— Henry Ford

Chapter 14 — Action Changes Facts

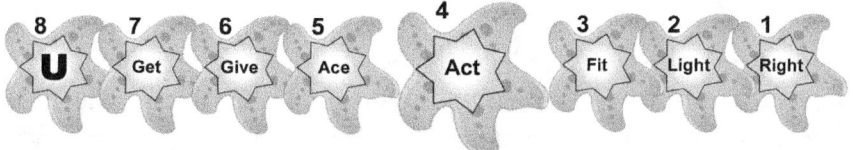

*"If we all do one random act of kindness daily,
we just might set the world in the right direction."*
— Martin Kornfeld

The previous chapter was our last look at changing our reactions from fear to love. In this chapter, we will change the energy of re-acting to doing or acting in situations, by removing the "F" and "S" from "facts" so the word becomes "act." The more we live with positive energy and become aware of how we are using our energy, the more we *act* before situations in our lives cause us to react. In everyday speech, we have sayings like: "Take action, take steps." Someone once said, "Life has no remote. Get up and change it yourself." As we are still travelling on the *love bus*, I like to say we *act* as *champions* for love instead of using *facts* as fear motivation.

Finding The Gift Going Through Tough Times

*"Beauty has so many forms, and I think the most beautiful
thing is confidence and loving yourself."*
— Kiesza

Can we break the pattern of reacting?

I often listen to grownups reacting to crying children. The normal response is, "You are fine dear, stop crying." That statement always reminds me of the colour turquoise, which symbolises hiding behind walls of protection so we do not feel the hurt. It is no wonder our grownup response to "How are you?" is usually, "I am fine, thank you."

I worked in nursery schools for a short while when I came to New Zealand and was intrigued to hear how quickly the children picked up on the negative behaviour in their friends and told them off. We teach our children to judge and to keep counting and scoring the negative in people.

Being brought up in such a domesticated environment, it is no surprise we focus on the negative. How would it change children if they were taught the power of words and that certain words have higher frequencies than others, instead of teaching them to make their friends feel guilty through blame and shame?

Being aware of the consequences and facts of domestication, can we start to *act* in different ways, like teaching our children with love and praise? Growing up with the knowledge your parents believe in you and trust you to *act* in the right way, makes it easier to make the *right* choices. Many parents, teachers, and caregivers already catch children when they do *right*.

Write Your Story:
- Are you one of the people catching children doing the right thing, or do you still catch them in the act of wrongdoing?
- Start to praise yourself and catch yourself making right choices and it will be mirrored to you on the outside through those around you.

Acting With Kindness Is Soul Food

"Your acts of kindness are iridescent wings of divine love,
which linger and continue to uplift others
long after your sharing."
— Rumi

What acts of kindness can you do during a day?

In Chapter 5, I had a whole list of *facts* on my *fear bus*. Learning to *act* with love and kindness on my *love bus*, I soon realised big *acts* were not needed to change my life. I like what Orison Swett Marden said, "Don't wait for extraordinary opportunities. Seize common occasions and make them great." As you have realised by now, I am a list maker.

Here is my list for *acts* of kindness:

1. Help to carry someone's parcels.

2. Be nice to people even if they are rude. It does not matter what they do — you are a nice person.

3. Smile when you walk past someone and greet him or her.

4. Send love to people in a group.

5. Give people a compliment even if you do not know them.

6. Let the person behind you go before you in a queue.

7. Hold a door open for someone.

8. Say, "Please", "Thank you", and "I am sorry." These words unlock people's hearts.

9. Tell people in shops, restaurants, and public toilets who clean up you appreciate them.

10. Write notes on the back of your business cards and leave them everywhere to show people you think they are special.

11. Pray for everybody involved when you hear an ambulance or fire truck passing.

Write Your Story:

•   Write down five acts of random kindness you plan to do today and then do them.

Acting Can Be One Moment At A Time

> *"Success is the sum of small efforts*
> *repeated day in and day out."*
> — R. Collier

Are you aware enough to seize the moment?

There is a beautiful story about an old man and his grandson who were very close. One morning the old man said to his grandson, "Today we are going to change the flow of the river." Reaching the river, they saw many stones in the shallow water. The old man walked into the shallow water, picked up a stone, put it on the bank of the river, and said to his grandson, "Now we can go home. Today we have changed the flow of the river."

One stone can change the flow of a river. In the beginning of my fear journey, I started changing the flow of my river with one moment of joy a day.

Write Your Story:

- Write down one small thing you are going to do in the next hour to change the flow of your river.

Change Your Attitude

In the word reveal of "boredom" is the sentence "Me do more" and combining letters in "bored" and "boring" we find the word "reborn." I am sure if people who complain about boredom have a purpose to live love and start to live a life of excellence, they will feel as if they are "reborn." Sai Baba said, "All action results from thought, so it is thoughts that matter." I often hear people remark the next generation is growing up in a world where their minds are ruled by technology instead of being earthed in the here and now. I think technology is a wonderful thing, and I always say Google is my friend, but I am shocked when people walk in the streets and cross a road without even looking up from their phones. We can tell our children and grandchildren about all the health dangers of an overload of technology, but it is up to them to make the decision to find balance in their own lives. As George Bernard Shaw said, "Progress is impossible without change, and those who cannot change their minds cannot change anything."

Write Your Story:

- Even if you don't do anything else today, write down how you are going to change your technology dependency to experience life in the now.

"To overcome the fear, all you need to do is to understand that there is fear and act anyway."
— Peter McWilliams

Have you ever had to make a decision to act when the facts you have were telling you not to?

Many years ago, a distress signal came in from a ship that got into trouble during a storm off the New England coast. A young member of the Coast Guard rescue mission said, "We can't go out; we'll never get back." The old captain replied, "We have to go out. We don't have to come back." That is what I will call *facing the facts*: acknowledging the *fear* and doing the *right* thing anyway.

Write Your Story:

- Do you have a story to tell about facing your fears and acting despite your fear?

Summary

Change your list of *facts* to a list of random *acts* of kindness. Then do one small *act* and see how quickly you change your life by making someone else's day beautiful.

To change from making a list of facts to acting on those facts, we first must change our attitude. We have to understand we cannot outrun our *shadow part* or our fear, but we can face our fears bravely and act in a wise and courageous way in the face of fear.

The Biggest Lessons

By *facing* our *fears*, we manage our energy, overcome our fear reactions, and change them into positive actions.

Word Reveal And The Power Of Words

While working with *action* and *facts*, I once again was reminded that we have the choice when we work with words to use a fact in fear or change that fact into a loving vibration.

Rainbow Blessing

It is with gratitude I express my power through God's power within me.

"The great aim of education is not knowledge, but action."
— Herbert Spencer

Chapter 15 — Acting As An Ace

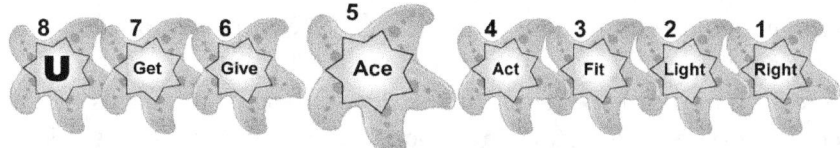

"We don't grow when things are easy;
we grow when we face challenges."
— Author Unknown

In Chapter 14, I talked about learning to *act* in love instead of reacting in fear. In Chapter 15, we use that skill and *act* as an *ace* in our own lives. The word reveal of Face without an "F" is "ace." The definition of an ace: a person who excels at a particular sport or other activity. Synonyms for *ace* are excellent, marvellous, wonderful, magnificent, outstanding, champion, master, star, and winner. It all fits in with the previous two chapters on how to get *fit* and live a life of excellence by outgrowing our own cells every day. When we start to live the true meaning of *cell*, we become the star and the winner in our own lives. Standing in our own power as masters of our lives, there is no need to compete against anyone. We know with an inner wisdom and quiet confidence we are capable of doing great things.

Make The Decision To Live Or Die

"A thousand times we die in one life. We crumble, break, and
tear apart until the layers of illusion are burned away and all
that is left is the truth of who and what we really are."
— Teal Scott

Have you ever had to make a decision between life and death?

Working through my own choices of life and death, I used to say I am not scared of death. It is the living part I have problems with. There comes a time while travelling on the desert road when you have to make a decision to live or die. Depression is not the only teacher leading to this choice. I strongly believe we cannot really live life fully every day unless we have made that decision.

I remember reading a story many years ago about a guy named Pete, who owned a restaurant. One morning, Pete forgot to lock the door behind him as he opened his restaurant, and the next moment, robbers were holding a gun to his head. He was so shocked and scared that his hands shook too much for him to open the safe. The robbers panicked and shot him. As he was lying on the ground, Pete saw in the eyes of the medics his condition was serious. Relating the story to a friend later, he said, "It was then I made the choice to live." As he was taken to the hospital and then rushed into the operating room, the looks on the faces around him convinced him his wounds must be life-threatening. As Pete was lifted onto the operating table, he asked the doctor to operate on him as if he was going to live. I am convinced his attitude to live made the difference.

Write Your Story:
- Have you had to make a decision to live or die?
- Often it is not so much a choice between life and death, but a choice to get out of the feeling of death and start living.

Managing My Energy In My Own Space

"If we are to have true peace in the world,
we must first find it within ourselves."
— Author Unknown

Do you have inner peace?

The word peace contains the word *ace*. To have peace in the world, we need to find our inner *ace* or our inner *space*. When I started my business in 1994, I called my courses Personal Space Management, which quickly became Energy Management in the business world. The next step was calling it ME, teaching people to Manage Energy, we first have to learn to work with our own energy.

I only started to understand the real meaning of my inner space when yoga taught me about the space between breaths, which is as important as the breath itself. It is like the spirit or soul you cannot see, but you know it is there. I have said before that I believe the breath is Spirit living in me. If I stop breathing, Spirit will have left my body. I use the example of the *fear* or *love bus* as the vehicle. Our bodies are the bus, and it can be filled with fear or love. Fear is the ego or shadow part, which is the personality saying, "I am a…" and then follows our whole resume.

Love is the space within that is left when we let go of fear and find the pureness and power of our inner peace. One of the most interesting observations in my own journey is when I am not at peace on the inside, there is chaos in my outside world. When we reach that inner space and peace, we do not have to tell people about it. They can see it in our actions as an *ace*.

Write Your Story:

- What are you doing to find your inner space and inner peace?

Becoming The Teacher

> *"I used to think great teachers inspire you.*
> *Now I think I had it wrong Good teachers inspire you;*
> *great teachers show you how to inspire yourself every day*
> *of your life. They don't show you their magic.*
> *They show you how to make magic of your own."*
> — Alfred Doblin

Have you accepted the possibility you are someone's teacher?

The first time I saw the above quote, I thought I would like to be that kind of a teacher. Although I have been in leadership positions, I have always taken the *Flighter* option with good excuses, like I am a better follower than a leader. However, Spirit had other plans for me. I realised I was being prepared to speak about fear and love and teach people the power of their thoughts and words, combining my teaching with the unique language of colour in the process. I mentioned before my fear was so strong, I refused to do the work. It was during one of my talks with Spirit, my name for God, with whom I often chat, that the Master told me, "You just turn up. We will do the rest." That helped me put my feet on the road to be a teacher of love. I still wholeheartedly agree with Socrates who said: "I cannot teach anyone anything. I can only make them think."

On my journey, I attended all the courses I possibly could about personal growth. It was only when I started teaching classes myself that I realised the difference between a student and a teacher. The student has very little responsibility. I have often said I only really understood what it was all about when I started to teach yoga instead of practicing yoga as a student. The teacher is the one who watches every student. This was made very clear to me during another personal experience. I helped a client work through a very difficult challenge. Due to circumstances, I found myself suffering some of the consequences. During a conversation with Spirit, I said it was not fair. It was not my lesson. The answer was very clear. "The teacher walks with the student. Jesus walked with his disciples while he was on Earth." Indeed, sometimes the teacher or therapist benefits and learns as much as the client.

Write Your Story:

- We are all teachers to someone. What are you teaching your followers?

Teaching The Truth Through Words

> "The pen is mightier than the sword."
> — Edward Bulwer-Lytton

The quote above is a good reminder that words are more powerful than weapons.

Looking for the truth hidden within "sword", it was no surprise to me to find "words."

Leo Buscaglia said, "A teacher gently leads you back to yourself." Finding myself more and more involved through my work as a healer and a teacher of awareness, I realised the words healer, teacher, and awareness all have ear in them, reflecting the importance of listening in these roles. I asked myself, "What kind of a teacher or healer do I want to be?" and "What am I supposed to listen to or hear?" What was the meaning for me to see the word ear in so many words? I got my answer during meditation — as the word meditations revealed the sentence:

"Sit in meditation and mind is tamed." I realised the meaning of *ear* for me was to get into that space deep inside my being to listen to my inner ear, or as I call it, to listen with God's ears.

Working on my Rainbow language, I made three words out of *ear*, namely *energy*, *awareness*, and *responsibility*. In Chapter 10, we learned about energy and that everything is energy.

The second letter in *ear* is for *awareness*. To become aware of what we think, feel, say, and do every moment gives us the opportunity and also the confidence to make choices. People who live or work in places where there is a lot of fear will have difficulty making choices. Where there is fear, there are few risk takers.

The fear of failure keeps many people from living their lives to the full. I like the saying, "Failures are part of life. If you don't fail, you don't learn. If you don't learn, you'll never change." We have to understand failure is not the opposite of success — it is part of success, and success without "U" (you) is not a word!

The last letter of *ear* is for *responsibility*. The story where Pete decided to live is a good example of taking responsibility for our own lives. Changing our vehicle from a *fear bus* to a *love bus* means we take responsibility for everything that happens to us. Leo Buscaglia said your life is your canvas. You paint the pictures on it, but if you don't like the picture, you cannot blame circumstances, your parents, or God. I say we have to take responsibility for our own lives and drive our own *love bus*. Leading the way and becoming an *ace* in our own lives is one of the biggest responsibilities we can take on. Looking at how irresponsible political leaders sometimes *act* makes me wonder how many of them listen with their *God ears*. Teaching the truth through words is a responsibility I have taken on to bring light into this world.

Note: My editor made me aware of the fact that many English words have "ear" in them. I think English is a Universal language and we should all start to listen to our words and what people are saying. Really listening to one another instead of playing political games, we may be able to build a better world for generations to come.

Write Your Story:

- What kind of responsibility have you taken on to make the world a better place?

Loving Fear Means Accepting Your Shadow

Are there circumstances in your life you cannot change?

Sometimes we have to accept the shadows in our lives instead of fighting to change them.

By now, you have realised the *fear* and *love bus*, are the sum total of our spiritual, mental, emotional, and physical bodies. We cannot run away or trade the *fear* bus for the *love* bus, and in the same way, we cannot trade our bodies for new ones. However, we can change our attitudes with the roadmap we have been exploring in this book.

We cannot get away from the fact that we live in a world of duality. It is our responsibility to find our truth in spite of duality. Only when we embrace the duality can we dance with our shadow instead of fighting with ourselves. In our world of duality, we talk about fear and love, light or the shadow part, life and death, give and receive. When I studied yoga and breathing techniques, I also learnt about unity and balance. To heal ourselves, we first acknowledge the facts about our lives, accept where we are, surrender — which means to be happy under any circumstances and to let go, which happens when we work through the process of forgiveness and learn self-love.

This may sound strange, but I had to learn to like my own birthday. As a child, my birthdays were always special. My mom would decorate my chair at the table, and although it was not like today where children get showered with gifts, it was a special day. To be honest, I have always been surrounded by people who made me feel special on my birthday, but I did not like to be fussed about.

Breaking away from the *chains* of the *fear bus* made me realise I had to learn to love the part of me that was happy to give but felt guilty when I received love. Only when I realised how wonderful it is that at a specific time, on a specific day, during a specific month a human being is born with the purpose of learning about love did I appreciate the wonder of a birthday. Whereas others are disappointed if they do not get presents, I had to learn the people who love me want to make my birthday special for me, and the gifts are, in fact, God showering me with grace.

Searching for the meaning of grace, I came upon a very interesting article from Jack Wellman. According to him, grace is from God and something we receive, but do not deserve. He uses the example of a birthday gift and says we do not deserve presents on our birthday, but we get them. We do not earn a birthday present, and we cannot force anybody to give us one. It is by the grace of the other person that we get the present. Believing there is a spark of God in every person, it makes perfect sense to me that on your birthday you are reminded about God's grace by loving people around you. I now appreciate that giving and receiving gifts is part of living life as an *ace*.

My dear friend Willa Vermooten, who lived to be a wise, 102-year-old light being, gave me a birthday wish that is so appropriate for this story.

"That which happens to you in life, try and cope with the situation as best you can and handle it with grace, because we are often so busy to fight against things that happen to us, instead of accepting and surrendering into the situation."

This wisdom came from one who became an *ace* in her own life and the lives of others through the grace of God. What an honour to have known such a teacher. I am grateful for the reminder that the gift of grace from God is the best way to love your shadow part.

Write Your Story:

- Are you listening to your inner voice?
- Is there a situation you cannot change and have to handle with grace?

Healing With Laughter

Honour all your facets; they are the light of your soul.

In Chapter 8, I told the story of the master who pushed his disciples over the edge and they flew. My life took on a whole new dimension after my husband and I moved to New Zealand. Finding my own space and matching my pace with the new energy to act as an ace in a new country took patience and time. One way I kept myself going in the strangeness of a new country was humour and laughter. Learning to work with my own fears during the 1980s and 1990s, I stumbled upon humour as a stress reliever. One of the many books I read about humour and healing with humour was *Anatomy of an Illness* by Norman Cousins. Cousins refused to accept the prognosis when diagnosed with ankylosing spondylitis (a chronic and progressive disease that would have made him an invalid). Cousins, with the help of his doctor, worked out his own therapy, which consisted of large doses of Vitamin C and laughter. He discovered ten minutes of belly laughs had an anaesthetic effect that gave him at least two hours of pain-free sleep. He watched as many funny videos as he could lay his hands on and laughed himself back to health. Following the trail of humour all over the world, through the books I read, I found enough evidence to believe humour is a good tool for healing and healthy living. Nobody can advise us to laugh off a serious illness, but many in the health care profession believe that humour therapy can be one of the best antidepressants freely available.

However, the main answer for self-healing came when Cousins wrote to Dr Albert Schweitzer asking how people could be healed by a witch doctor. Dr Schweitzer's answer was, "The witch doctor succeeds for the same reason all the rest of us succeed. Each patient carries his own doctor inside him. They come to us not knowing that truth. We are at our best when we give the doctor who resides within each patient a chance to go to work." I have worked with this concept as a healer for many years, honouring the patient and the God Power inside him or her.

Living a life of excellence and being an *ace* in your own and others' lives is made easier by humour. I find humour is a wonderful motivational tool for enhancing productivity in companies. It is far more effective than using fear words like restructuring, layoffs, or takeovers that breed fear, resulting in employee insecurity that ultimately leads to hostility and other reactions no company can afford.

Companies using humour as one of their cornerstones when building a culture of excellence find reductions in sick leave and burnout as a result. People who are relaxed and not fearful communicate better; they are able to manage conflict through creative problem solving and will be motivated to take risks, which fearful people will not do.

Going on the humour trip, you have to understand the humour I talk about is many times a word as misinterpreted as love. Humour is not being a "class clown" or a "stand-up comedian." It is definitely not about teaching people who do not have humour to be funny; rather, it is about learning to anticipate situations where humour might help to resolve a difficult situation.

The saying "You cannot have a belly laugh and be angry at the same time" is very true. I use a pot to put the "stuff " in, but using humour is another way of distancing yourself from a problem. One of the main things I had to learn was to laugh at myself. I was far too serious about life. Using humour techniques made my life lighter. The quote "Laughter is the shortest distance between two people" is one of my favourites. Creating a humour pool in the workplace where everyone can contribute positive humour is one way to start bringing humour into the workplace. Always remember sarcasm is not humour. In fact, it leads to revenge and is fear motivating.

One of my favourite slides in my humour presentation states:

"Research shows the first five minutes of life are very risky. The last five minutes are not so hot either. It is what happens between the first and the last five minutes of life that makes the difference."

Write Your Story:
- Write down one or two situations you could lighten with humour.
- Maybe you would like to start by watching a funny movie or video to first get your humour triggered.

Summary
One of the most important steps to becoming an *ace* in my own life was to choose between life and death. Making that decision changed my life from living in fear and concentrating on the negative, to a life lived in love, shifting my focus to the positive. Every person is a teacher in someone's life. We have to ask ourselves whether we are influencing people in a positive or negative way. I decided to teach people about the *light* messages within words and to be aware of the power of the words we use.

Some situations we cannot change, so we have to learn to love our shadow parts through acceptance.

Living a life of excellence and using humour as one of the cornerstones can heal people on many levels — it is one of the best stress relievers.

The Biggest Lessons

An *ace* has the wisdom to know that a life lived in gratitude and love happens through the grace of God.

Word Reveal And The Power Of Words

A word reveal of *Face* is "ace." In *space* and *peace*, we also find ace. Balance, accept, and circumstances all have ace in them. The word reveal of grace is ace, ear, race, care. Facets — acts, as, ace. These power words each tell their own story of how we act as an ace.

Rainbow Blessing

Blessings of inner peace flow into our lives through the grace of God.

Chapter 16 — Giving With Gratitude

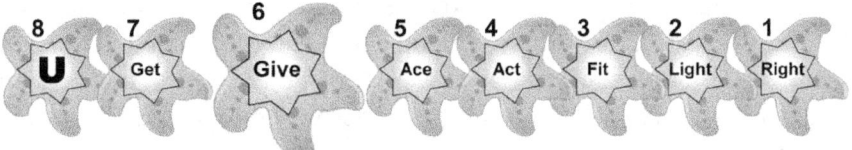

"Forgiveness is the final form of love."
— Reinhold Niebuhr

The previous chapter was about changing our circumstances and acting as an ace in our own lives and the lives of others. In this chapter, we will work with one of the twins, namely *forgive* and what happens when we live forgiveness and move forward as champions of love.

Forgiveness can be defined as: The intentional and voluntary process by which a victim undergoes a change in feelings and attitude regarding an offense; letting go of negative emotions, such as vengefulness, with an increased ability to wish the offender well.

Starting With Self-Love Can Lead To An Extraordinary Life

"Everyone wants to lead an extraordinary life."
— Augustus Caesar

How are you doing with self-love?

Mercy is a word I associate with forgiveness. The word reveal in mercy is "me, cry." When we have done something wrong, we normally expect to be punished. Instead of receiving the expected punishment, when shown compassion or forgiveness, I have seen people cry with gratitude. There are many stories, especially in religious books, about mercy and grace. I best relate to stories and the lessons in the Bible about mercy. We see God's mercy in the story of Jonah, who delivered God's message to the city of Nineveh to repent or be destroyed. In learning to live a life of love, we also have to learn the meaning of mercy and show mercy in our lives. Jonah did not expect the people to repent, so he sat outside the city to watch the destruction, which did not happen. God sent him shade in the form of a plant, and then destroyed the plant to teach Jonah a valuable lesson in mercy. When Jonah complained to God about the loss of his shade, God said to Jonah that he was angry about losing his shade, but the real reason for his anger was because God showed mercy towards the people of Nineveh. Jonah had to learn that even if we deserve to be punished, when we repent and ask for forgiveness, mercy follows. One of the lessons when working through the process of forgiveness is, in spite of justified punishment, to show mercy frees all of us from the chains of fear.

Louise Hay said, "The act of forgiveness takes place in our own mind. It really has nothing to do with the other person." Showing mercy to others by forgiving them when they have wronged us is an act of kindness towards ourselves — helping to heal ourselves from holding on to the poison of unforgiveness and being an ogre in our own lives.

Forgiveness is the best form of love. It takes a strong person to say: "I am sorry" and an even stronger person to forgive. If you are working on self-love and have to say to yourself, "I am sorry. I messed up my life and the lives of many other people", then look at yourself in the mirror and say, "It is okay. I forgive you." That is a *wow* moment in any person's life.

To live life as an ace does not mean you are super-rich or living a life without challenges. Thinking lovable and loving thoughts about yourself is a good beginning. For many people, to say kind and loving words to themselves may be their exceptional performance for that day. The good thoughts will grow and escalate in your mind. Soon the light in you will overflow into the outside world, and you will start to look at people around you with soft eyes — and you will find yourself doing random acts of unexpected service for others. It can be something as small as a smile and a friendly "good morning" to a stranger passing by. Even if the person does not answer back, your heart will sing its own song to you.

Write Your Story:

There is truth in saying that sadness and tragedy come to us so we can learn about love. In difficult times we change and learn the truth about forgiveness. C. S. Lewis said, "Hardship often prepares an ordinary person for an extraordinary destiny."

- Write about something you have done today to show self-love and to make yourself feel extraordinary.

Unlocking Abundance With Gratitude

"Gratitude is our ability to see the grace of God,
morning by morning, no matter what else greets us
in the course of the day."

— Craig Barnes

Have you given yourself the gift of an attitude of gratitude? As a child, I loved to sing the song in church with the chorus:

Count your blessings, name them one by one.
Count your blessings, see what God has done.
Count your blessings, name them one by one.
And it will surprise you what the Lord has done.

Deepak Chopra said, "Gratitude opens the door to the power, the wisdom, and creativity of the universe. You open the door through gratitude."

I have always found it easy to give and never gave a second thought to how the receiver might feel. It was only when I found myself on the receiving end that I realised I needed to forgive myself for sometimes giving in an uncaring manner. When you are in a position where people give to you, emotions of guilt and shame can surface. Now when I give to people, I do it with a blessing and humility, almost in reverence for the honour of being allowed to give. In Mother Teresa's words, "It's not how much we give, but how much love we put into giving."

One of my clients taught me a wonderful lesson in giving. She pays me more than I charge for a session. Jim Fargiano says, "Gratitude and love are always multiplied when you give freely. It is an infinite source of contentment and prosperous energy."

Write Your Story:

- Without thinking too much, take three minutes to write about all the things for which you are grateful.

Walking Your Path

I believe we all choose our own lessons and every person who comes into our lives is a teacher. Sometimes the ones we hate the most are, in fact, our greatest teachers. We have to find the spiritual lesson in every situation. It is not about the difficult boss or the partner who abuses or leaves us. We have to learn a lesson or master a lower vibration before we can move to a higher frequency — almost like going to a higher grade in school. To reach our full potential and unite with our higher selves, we have to let go of lower vibrations. Hate, anger, judgement, jealousy, revenge, unforgiveness, and all fear-induced thoughts, feelings, words, and actions keep us from achieving this goal.

I hope you have worked with me on this journey to let go of the lower vibrations. The choice to give yourself and others the gift of freedom through forgiveness unleashes the spark of hope in your heart, and instead of separation and fear, we have a life of unity and love with God.

> *"And now these three remain: faith, hope, and love.*
> *But the greatest of these is love."*
> — 1 Corinthians 13:13

Let faith, hope, and love be your luggage on the love bus, instead of shame, blame, and guilt. When we have those bags, it is easy to give thanks for a week of love and miracles coming to us and unknown blessings we are awaiting with excitement. It is easy to give our love to those who don't deserve it because we know we are living in God's grace. Martin Luther King, Jr. said: "Forgiveness is not an occasional act; it is a permanent attitude."

Write Your Story:

- Who or what is your biggest challenge on your journey?
- Will it help you to start to see this challenge as a lesson, and if there are people involved, to see them as your teachers?

Holding The Rope

*"At times our own light goes out and is rekindled by a spark
from another person. Each of us has cause to think with deep
gratitude of those who have lighted the flame within us."*
— Albert Schweitzer

Would you like to know how to be a rope holder?

It is natural to share and serve others, giving of yourself when you have been regenerated by the grace of God. I would like to end this chapter with a story that inspired me to write my own story called "Holding the Rope."

Someone told me a story about a very rare and precious plant that grew on the highest peak of a mountain. It flowered once a year during a full moon, and the people of the neighbouring areas believed the flower had healing properties. The problem was many people lost their lives trying to get to the flower.

The plant grew on the highest peak underneath a rock overhang that was always covered with ice and snow. Fierce winds constantly roared over the mountaintop, making it almost impossible to climb back up from the sharp overhang where the plant grew. Many strong and accomplished mountaineers lost their lives trying to get the flower.

The town itself was dying since no one wanted to live where so many people had lost their lives. One day, a very wealthy man came to the town and said if the townsfolk would get him the flower, he would make the town a wonderful place again.

A small boy immediately said he would go, but the people said no. They would rather all perish than let the boy risk his life. The boy argued that he was small and light and he could easily go over the edge with a rope and be pulled back up. The people were steadfast in their refusal, but the boy said, "I am not afraid. I will go if my daddy holds the rope." The boy was not scared because he trusted the rope holder completely. This is the basis for me telling people I am holding the rope for them.

In times of hardship, it is comforting to know that someone is anchoring for you.

I loved the story, but I wanted my own version of the rope holder. I asked God to show me a picture of the words "holding the rope for someone." I received the following vision:

I see the form of a woman. She is standing on a rock, her face turned towards the sea. The wind is blowing through her hair, and her dress, wet from the spray, is clinging to her small figure. The thundering waves roll towards her, breaking close by. There is a rope flowing from her hands into the sea. A relaxed smile plays around her lips; her soft eyes scan the waters in front of her, peering deep into the sea. She knows a person is clinging to the rope. Sometimes there is more than one person. These people are not weak; they can get out of the sea on their own if they know someone believes in them. Maybe they are going through a dark, scary night of sickness, death, or loneliness. In the sea of life, there are many fearful and scary storms. The people in the stormy sea can see the rope holder standing on the rock, and they experience the comfort and love of someone who cares. That is why she is standing on the rock being a beacon of light to those who need love and support.

I ask the question, "Lord, the woman is so small against the mighty waters. What happens if she gets tired?"

The scene changes — I suddenly see behind the woman a mighty Angel. Now I understand why the rope comes out of her hands and she is not holding it. It is pure energy flowing through her. She is standing on that rock, with a mighty Angel behind her. When she gets tired, she leans back against the Angel and he enfolds her in his powerful cloak of protection. They stand on that rock, the mighty Angel and the small woman. When she leans back against the Angel, she knows with certainty no one will be lost, because the sea of life is full of Angels and people standing on rocks holding ropes. They stand there as long as they are needed.

We all have times when we are in the sea of life — even the rope holders go through troubled times and need someone holding the rope for them. The words of Galatians 6:2 came to me: "Carry each other's burdens, and in this way you will fulfil the law of Christ." Through this vision, I understood how we hold the rope of energy for one another. I bowed my head in awe and gratitude for the holy and sacred meal that was served to me.

Write Your Story:

- Can you think of someone who is in the sea of life who you can hold the rope for?
- Maybe you want to relate a story of how someone held a rope for you.

Summary

Showing mercy towards others by forgiving them when they have wronged us is an act of kindness towards ourselves. We unlock the doors of abundance on many levels through gratitude. With an attitude of forgiveness, we take the luggage of faith, hope, and love on the journey of love with us.

Forgiving is giving forward with love. When we give the gift of forgiveness, we are like someone holding a rope for the people who are still struggling in the sea of life.

The Biggest Lessons

Forgiveness is an act of self-love because it happens in our mind. Forgiveness is not a one-off act — it is an attitude.

Word Reveal And The Power Of Words

Word Reveal: Forgive — for, give. In Chapter 7's word reveal, I showed you that the most important negative word revealed, if we do not forgive and forget, is ogre. The definition of an ogre is a monster that eats human flesh. Without forgiveness, we can poison ourselves and hatred can eat us from the inside.

It is important when becoming a *Star* or a *Champion* that through *giving* we remember *forgiveness* is a way of living. After all these years, I still find myself at the end of a day forgiving myself for not treating my body with love all the time either through a thought, feeling, or a word.

Rainbow Blessing

Let mercy and gratitude follow our act of forgiveness.

"And think not you can direct the course of love,
for love, if it finds you worthy, directs your course."
— Kahlil Gibran, The Prophet

Chapter 17 — Receiving With Grace

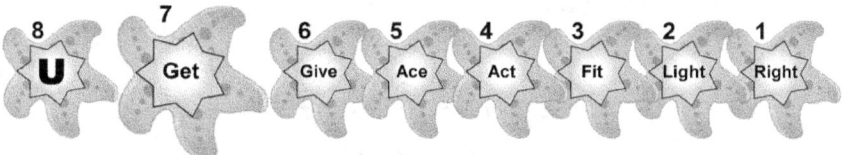

"Happiness cannot be travelled to, owned, earned, worn, or consumed. Happiness is the spiritual experience of living every minute with love, grace, and gratitude."
— Denis Waitley

In Chapter 16, we started to reveal our truth as we worked with forgiveness and started to give love to ourselves and others. Chapter 17 is about what happens when we work with the word "get."

Receiving Peace

"Inner peace begins the moment you choose not to allow another person or event to control your emotions."
— Author Unknown

Do you have inner peace?

One of the gifts you can put in your luggage on the *love bus* is the inner peace you will feel when you have worked through forgive and forget.

Someone once said you have to go down on your knees, and from there you can find forgiveness. I say unless you plug into the God Source, you cannot forgive and forget. It is the higher energy that moves us through the situations in our lives, causing us trauma and pain. It is a choice we make to let go. Louise Hay said, "I choose to make the rest of my life the best of my life." Having made the choice, our lives change, and we receive inner peace. I love the saying, "Peace is seeing the sunrise or a sunset and knowing whom to thank."

Write Your Story:

- Write how you got to your point of inner peace and quiet.

Receiving As You Give

> *"Every act of kindness benefits the giver
> as well as the receiver."*
> — Katrina Mayer

Do you often feel you receive as much as you give and more?

Exercise — Learning about the Power of Our Words

The following exercise should be done with another person. You do not have to know the person well. In fact, the less you know the better. Write a word to describe your partner as you perceive him or her. Write down a strength you see in that person and something you think he or she can change or work on. Share what you have written. Allow the other person to share what he or she has written about you. You may realise what you say about the other person other people can also say about you, or you may already know you are like that. We cannot see anything in other people if it is not already in us. Therefore, we can stop judging or blaming others and start to act in kind ways towards ourselves and others. Keeping this exercise in mind, you will soon find if you give with an open heart, you will receive from others as much love as you give.

It is also good to remember every time you say something bad about someone, you are badmouthing yourself. There is a saying: "Energy flows where energy goes." I say energy glows where it flows and choosing to light up the world giving and receiving love is the greatest gift we can give.

Write Your Story:

- Did you learn something about the words you use and what they say about you?
- Write a few lines on your experience with this exercise.

Getting Answers From The Young

"When I approach a child, he inspires in me two sentiments,
tenderness for what he is and respect
for what he may become."
— Louis Pasteur

Do you think children can be your teachers?

One of my young clients is a lively ten-year-old boy with a wonderful sense of humour and a good shot of innocent mischief, which has landed him in a few tight spots. He is, like many young children today, a highly spiritual soul — which at ten is seen as spirited instead of spiritual, or the current favourite word, hyperactive. I have been working with him for three years now, and a few weeks ago, he told me how much I have helped him to change from being "hyper" to being able "to handle his extra energy as well as his anger."

Recently, this young man got a lesson in trust, or rather in what happens when someone you trust breaks that trust. Discussing the situation, I told him about some of the techniques I use in my work as a spiritual coach, and we discussed forgiveness and forgetting. He said he did not know how to get the situation out of his mind. I explained why it would stay with him, but that working with forgiveness and learning to forget would mean that when he thought about the situation or saw the person, he would have no emotional charge anymore. I also told him the person is only one of his many teachers in life, and sometimes the people who hurt us the most can be our greatest teachers.

We worked with the wonderful technique of Ho'oponopono, and I told him how to say, "I'm sorry", "Please forgive me", "Thank you", and offer a heartfelt "I love you." We did a mind map letter where he chose from three different faces how he felt when he heard the first time what his friend did to him. My brave young client looked into his own heart and said he was sorry about his role and asked his Higher Self to forgive him. He said, "Thank you" and told himself the words, "I love you." He signed his letter, folded it, and put it in the "forgiving pot." I told him he could reread his letter or leave it there, and every time he thinks about the situation he could use the technique I showed him. He will know when he has it out of his system. I told him, "In forgiveness is the word give. You are giving yourself the chance to learn and move on and enjoy the friendship with the person again if you choose to." In his case, the people involved didn't even know what they had done to him.

I also said, "In forget is the word get." He looked at me with those big, wise eyes and said, "Can I be angry a little bit longer. I will tell you when I *get* it, and we can burn the letter."

The way he caught on to my explanation of the meaning of words and said when he "gets it" made perfect sense to me. We have to *get* it that our ego can make us feel important and keep us the victim if we do not bring love and God's grace into *forgive* and *forget*.

In his book *The Fred Factor*, Mark Sanborn told the story of another boy who learned to "get" it. On Mark's son Hunter's first day in pre-kindergarten, Hunter asked his father, "Dad, what's the most important thing of all?" Impressed with his question, Mark told him, "Obey the teachers, learn as much as you can, and play well with the other kids." Hunter interrupted his father with exasperation and said, "The most important thing of all is love."

Write Your Story:

- Did you *get* it, or are you still working through *forgive and forget*?
- Give and get are the gifts you receive when you have mastered the skill to forgive and forget.
- Write your story.

Summary

You give yourself the gift to move on with life if you forgive, and when you think of the person or situation and you have no emotional charge, you know you got it right. Letting go of anger and fear always results in a deep inner peace.

It will benefit us to remember we receive what we give, and when we give out negative vibrations like judging or blaming others, we will receive it also. We cannot say anything good or bad about another person if it is not already in us.

It is, therefore, important to realise everything happens inside our minds, and to heal ourselves and others, we can say the words "I am sorry", "Please forgive me", "Thank you", and "I love you" to our Higher Self.

The Biggest Lessons

Giving and getting is the gift hiding inside our hearts, waiting to be unlocked through the keys of forgive and forget.

Word Reveal And The Power Of Words

Word Reveal: Forget — for, get. *Forgiveness* is what we do *for* ourselves. Peace and freedom is the gift we *receive (get)* when living love as a champion.

Rainbow Blessing

Bless the children of this world.

"If we allow our 'high creativity' to remain alive, we will never be bored. We can pray, standing in line at the super market. Or we can be lost in awe at all the people around us, their lives full of glory and tragedy, and suddenly we will have the beginnings of a painting, a story, a song."

— Madeleine L'Engle.

Chapter 18 — Finding Fun – Finding Me

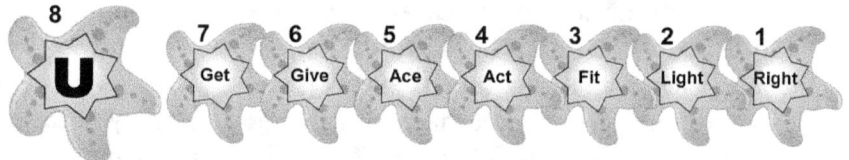

"Life teaches you the art of letting go in every event. When you have learnt to let go you will be joyful, and as you start being joyful more will be given to you."

— Sri Sri

In the last two chapters, we dealt with *give* and *get*. This chapter is about *ME*, which means *My Energy*. There are many ways to describe your life when you have come this far on the *love bus*, for example, living a life of excellence, living an extraordinary life, and being an ace are but a few. One of the lessons many people have to learn is to be happy and joyful amidst the everyday chaos we create through misperceptions. In the years that followed my healing and working as a spiritual coach, I realised the roadmap of the *fear chain* and *love stars* I used to heal myself benefitted many other people.

One of the words that can be associated with fun is enjoyment. The synonyms for joy are happiness, bliss, and ecstasy. Many years ago, I watched a live broadcast of Leo Buscaglia. One of the questions he asked his audience was, "Do you know what ecstasy feels like?" It took me a long time to understand the meaning of that question. Bliss for me was learning to let go of struggling through life on the fear bus. I found the tune to my own heart on the love bus, and now I share that joy as I dance through life. Melanie Koulouris said, "There is no sense in punishing your future for the mistakes of your past. Forgive yourself, grow from it, and then let it go."

Inner Laughter

"Always laugh when you can. It is cheap medicine."

— Lord Byron

Do you laugh on the inside when you cannot laugh out loud?

Realising everything happens in the mind and we create our world with our thoughts, I created a picture of a little, white-haired man with a long beard inside my head, and I named him Bao, which means "treasure" in Chinese. I am convinced he is a facet of me who lived and worked in the rice fields in an earlier life. Bao is my humour "funny bone." The things I find funny and cannot share with anybody are always a source of silent, inner laughter between Bao and me. When it is not appropriate to laugh or share my humour, I see him in my mind's eye. His eyes are closed, with many wrinkles around them, and he has an infectious laugh that comes from deep inside him. He enjoys the moment, while I stand there with a poker face. My sense of humour is not always funny for others, and therefore, my inner humour counterpart is a constant companion sharing my sense of humour.

Write Your Story:

- Do you have a funny story you can share reminding yourself to have fun?

ME=EM

What is in a name?

I mentioned in the Preface that these 4 letters became the basis for my ME teachings. Trying to make a personal signature out of the word "ME" brought me to a much deeper spiritual meaning for those 4 letters. In letters to family and friends I started signing my name in Afrikaans in such a way that it can be read backwards to remind myself I should always try to stay the same under all circumstances. By playing with the word me in English and making it meem, I wondered whether there is such a word. Once again my friend Google came to my rescue. According to urbandictionary.com, "Meem is a woman who is blonde and beautiful. Most meems seem to have green eyes. Meems are…great at making baked treats. You should find yourself a meem, but good luck finding one, most of them are married…." The description had me and my inner "humour man" chuckling for a while.

However, I learnt having fun on the love bus, being aware of who you really are when all the fears are gone, is to see the deeper meaning behind your fun. In Arabic, meem has a very deep spiritual meaning. Reading articles and explanations about the "M" or the word Meem in Arabic once again made me aware of the sacredness of some words. Taking the spiritual meaning into consideration, the word "Meem" took on a new meaning for me. Talking about "ME" (My Energy) in "Rainbow Language", "M" is for the breath of God in all of us. "E" is for Energy in all of us. Now every time I sign my name as *Meem* in my private letters, I am reminded that my heart beats with the rhythm of the "OM" sound and every breath is a gift from God.

Om (or Aum) is used in yoga and is considered the most sacred mantra in Hinduism and Tibetan Buddhism. In Sanskrit, it is seen as the "cosmic sound" and a very important symbol in yoga. To focus the mind on the word and contemplate its sacredness is a revered practice in many cultures. The word is viewed as the power from which the universe originated. It is seen by many as the sound of God.

Henri Le Saux (Swami Abhishiktananda), a Christian monk, said the following about the mantra "OM": "OM cannot be recommended indiscriminately to Christians, or of course to any others. It is too rich and too exalted for anyone to be capable of using it unless s/he has at least begun to taste the inner experience to which it refers. Otherwise, it remains an empty sound, having no spiritual echo in the one who utters it." Personally, Le Saux feels Psalm 46:10 sums it up best: "Be still, and know that I am God."

This once again focused my awareness on using the words "I am" and "ME" They can take on a very different meaning when we are on the love bus, reminding us of how unique and special we are in God's eyes.

Write Your Story:

- Do you have a story you can share reminding you of who you really are?

Staying Young At Heart With Magic, Miracles, And Me

> *"Some day you will be old enough*
> *to start reading fairy tales again."*
> — C. S. Lewis

Do you see the wonder of life around you every day?

When looking for synonyms for the word magic, I found enchanted, fairylike, and thrilling. I am always enchanted when I am in nature, especially walking in the forests and parks in New Zealand, where there is a fairylike beauty. Watching the sunrise or the moon over the bay from our lounge window never fails to be a thrilling experience for me.

The word miracle means wonder. In the word reveal of miracle is ear, real, clear, are, arc, ace, me. I made the sentence "I am a miracle." What a wonderful reminder within the word is a sentence to remind us who we really are. Playing with the words, I wrote: As an *ace*, I listen with my inner *ear*, anchoring the *arc* of the rainbow colours within *me* and I am *clear* about the *real me*.

I like to go for walks in the forest close to where we live. I recently had the joy of taking a mom and three children into the forest with me. It was the first time the little girl of five walked in a forest. Whenever I take people into the forest, I tell them the coloured stickers on the trees are fairy letters, and we often have great fun making up messages from the fairies. The wonder in this young girl's eyes when I read the first fairy letter was magical. I told her you have to see it in your heart to be able to read the fairy letters, and many people cannot see it, but little children still believe in the beauty of life and they can read it.

She grabbed her mother's hand and they were off looking for another fairy letter. When she saw the little coloured sticker, everybody had to gather around her to hear what the fairy letter said. "We love you, and you must come visit our forest again", she read to us.

The little girl skipped off holding her cousin's hand just as her sister, who is eleven, came up to me. She is very aware of her responsibility to be a good example to her little sister. She told me she could not see anything on the sticker and wanted to know whether I was making it all up. She was very worried I was not telling the truth. I told her our choices — we can walk through the forest with earphones on and run up and down the steps seeing and hearing very little of what is going on, or we can breathe in the beauty that is all around us. I can look at the stickers on the trees and see the nails in the trees or I can see a fairy letter.

I told her about the process where we teach children not to believe in magic and miracles because most of the time, we cannot see them.

We can also become so judgmental that we miss all the beauty, while concentrating on right or wrong. I told her there are people who can see the beings of the Elemental Kingdom, and I can feel their energy. Albert Einstein said, "There are two ways you can live your life. One is as though nothing is a miracle. The other is as if everything is a miracle." This story has a beautiful ending. Two years later, this girl, now age thirteen, was living one of my favourite quotes from Einstein: "Imagination is more important than knowledge." She wrote her little sister, now seven, a "real fairy letter" with so much love and imagination she even touched the hearts of the grownups in her family.

Write Your Story:

- Are you surrounded by magic and miracles?
- Make a list of all the wonderful things you can see in an hour during your day. Dr Wayne W. Dyer said in his book *I Can See Clearly Now*, "There is a secret garden where miracles and magic abound, and it's available to anyone who makes the choice to visit there."

Living Happily Ever After

"To experience peace does not mean that your life is always blissful. It means that you are capable of tapping into a blissful state of mind amidst the normal chaos of a hectic life."

— Jill Bolte Taylor

Are you happy with your life?

In Chapter 5, I said nobody tells you how to live happily ever after. I like to agree with Doe Zantamata, who says, "First bliss comes naturally. Second bliss is a choice. It's the choice to trust, to love, to put yourself out there, knowing full well that you can get hurt. But you won't be able to live, love, and experience all the joys of life if you don't put yourself back out there again. It takes courage — a lot of courage — but it's worth it."

As children, we trust and love unconditionally, until someone hurts us. The process of forgiving and forgetting can take us a long time, and sometimes we never recover from the pain and hurt. Holding on to the negative things keeps us from happiness. We may go from one relationship to the next, hoping to find happiness, but unless we heal ourselves first, nothing will change.

Write Your Story:

- Write a few lines on how you might find ways to live happily ever after with yourself.

Showing Respect To Others Is Saying A Lot About Me

"Good manners are just a way of showing other people that we have respect for them."
— Bill Kelly

Do you agree treating people with respect means you have dignity or self-respect?

I do not remember a lot about my mother's father, who was the only grandfather I knew as a child. I was ten when he died. I do remember he was a very dignified man. My mom told me a story about him that has stayed with me. At the end of his life, my grandfather had diabetes and had to have both of his legs amputated. In spite of the painful and very traumatic situation my grandfather was in, the nursing staff at the hospital spoke about his impeccable manners and the respect with which he treated them. It was only when I started to study the importance of good manners and the code of conduct of people living love that I realised he treated people with respect because he had respect for himself.

Living a life of excellence means we cannot compromise on good manners and respect. Goethe said, "A man's manners are a mirror in which he shows his portrait." I have written a story for my grandchildren in which I say there are keys they can use to open almost any door in life. They are *hello, goodbye, please, thank you,* and *I am sorry.*

Write your story:

- Make a list of what you see as good manners, or write a story describing how you feel about respect.

Summary

To find happiness we have to learn to let go of struggles on the *fear bus.* It is good if we can see ourselves in a lighter mood. Start to do things that keep you young at heart. Appreciating the beauty in nature and the wonder of our own uniqueness are the miracles that make our lives exciting.

It is a choice every moment of every day to live in a state of bliss. People who are on a frequency of love have a code of conduct that includes good manners and respect for all living beings.

In summary, I wrote this paragraph about the words on the *love bus:*

When starting to do the *right* things for yourself, life becomes *light,* and as your energy increases positively, you become a shining *light* for others. If you are a *fighter,* you will always be one, but if you learn to *fight* in the *right* way, you start to *act* as an *ace* in your own life and the lives of others. You *give* and you *get* so many positive things in your life. On your love journey through life, you have real *fun,* because your life is filled with success, joy, happiness, respect — the components of love and the real "U."

The biggest lessons

Letting go of old, outdated beliefs and habits and finding the fun in life brings out the real "U."

Word Reveal And The Power Of Words

Word Reveal: Fun — Looking at the word fun, I realised I had no fun. In fact, I did not know what fun was. I took away the F in fun and was left with "un," which is mostly used to describe something negative — unhappy, or as one of my students once said, "un-fun." Taking away the "N" left the U. I realised that *fun* is all about "U" (you), and like love, it has different meanings for all of us.

The word miracle means wonder. In the word reveal of miracle, there is ear, real, clear, are, arc, ace, and me. I also made from it the sentence "I am a miracle." What a wonderful reminder that within the word we have a sentence to remind us who we really are. Playing with the words, I wrote: As an *ace,* I listen with my inner *ear,* anchoring the *arc* of the rainbow colours within *me,* and I am *clear* about the *real me.*

Rainbow Blessing

May you master the art of letting go of all that is holding you back from living a joyful life.

Chapter 19
— Healing With Divine Rainbow Colours

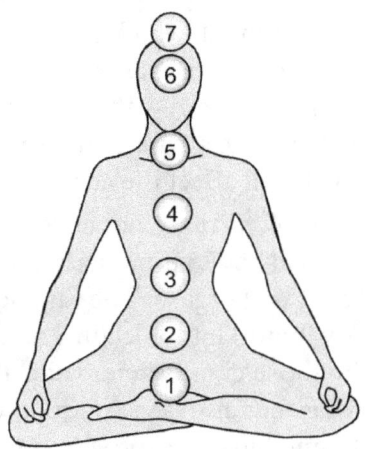

Rainbow Colours and Energy Centres

1. Red 2. Orange 3. Yellow 4. Green 5. Blue 6. Indigo 7. Violet

"God puts rainbows in the clouds so that each of us
— in the dreariest and most dreaded moments
— can see a possibility of hope."

— Maya Angelou

Chapter 18 was all about the *fun* I now create for *ME* on the *love bus*. In this chapter, we will focus on a hobby that became part of my life, my business, and my passion. The whole spectrum of colour healing is covered in detail during my training courses. At the end of this chapter, I will give you a taste of the meaning of colour as a blessing.

Our Energy System (Chakras)

In Chapter 6, I said I would give more information on the chakras.

Everyone has an invisible energy system called "chakras." Chakra is a Sanskrit word meaning "wheel or circle of light." The seven chakras are positioned from the base of the spine to the top of the head. Five

175

of the major chakras are in alignment with the spine, while the sixth is located between the eyebrows and the seventh is just above the crown of the head.

The chakras look like a funnel, which is narrow closest to the body and wider away from the body. The chakra is "blocked, weak, or frozen" when the energy flow is restricted — thereby causing disease. When balanced, the chakras spin like a wheel, creating an electromagnetic field. These characteristics all affect the auric field.

The chakras are located along the major endocrine glands that play an important role in the human body, i.e. pituitary, pineal, thyroid, pancreas, adrenal, and gonads or sexual organs. The functions and development of those glands are very important for leading a healthy life because the hormones secreted by those glands determine a person's mental and emotional mood. Those glands also have control over our energy, activity, psychological security, and biological process. More importantly, those glands have an effect on our actions, present conditions, body shape, and mentality. The chakras, therefore, play a major role in stimulating those glands, supplying them with energy, and keeping them intact and active. The energy is distributed to the whole body through the *meridians*.

Meridians can be described as channels of awareness acting as a medium to transfer energy throughout the organs of the human body. They look like arteries and veins that transfer blood. Meridians extend from the head to the feet. There are twelve main meridians in the body, each associated with an organ system.

We also get meridians in the bodies of mammals like cats, dogs, horses, and most importantly, the Earth.

Health troubles start taking place when one of the Meridians has a blockage. When a Meridian gets blocked, the energy cannot flow within the organs connected with it. It is the same as a clot in an artery. Depending on the degree of the blockage, energy health problems surface in the organs affected.

When your *energy* is leaking, weak, or frozen, you feel depleted, heavy, and even stuck. Energy-depletion makes it more difficult to manage your emotions, think positive thoughts, stay healthy, and attract harmony into your life.

Our *energy* responds very quickly when we know what to do to correct it.

Drinking From The Colours Of The Rainbow

"Let me, O let me bathe my soul in colours;
let me swallow the sunset and drink the rainbow."
— Kahlil Gibran

Do you like to look at the sunsets and rainbows like I do?

When still in South Africa, I was walking my dog Saint one day, and looking up — while in deep conversation with Spirit — saw a rainbow. That's when the words *Rainbow Divinity* came to me. I immediately knew that was the name for my business to do healing work.

From childhood, I have always been intrigued by rainbows, and I have never met anybody who did not like to look at one. Working with the light and the colours from my soul as I acknowledged the Presence of God within me, I spread those divine rainbow colours far and wide. Hope, faith, love, gratitude, and serving others are the colours I use to paint my life and to heal myself and many others who have travelled with me on the *fear and love bus* through the years. As I grow older, I am purposefully trying to create my life as a piece of art, and with Spirit's guidance, I am choosing the colours for my canvas every day. Someone once told me that it seems as if I have no problems, which I saw as a compliment, but it also brought a smile to my face. Healing, excellence, living an extraordinary life — it does not matter what we call it, choosing to live a life of love is an ongoing process; we have to work at it diligently every day.

Write Your Story:

• How are you going to colour your life with the beauty of colour and words?

Treating The Spirit Heals The Body

Are you ready to colour your life with the colours of your spirit?

I love Marianne Williamson's statement, "The spiritual journey is the unlearning of fear and the acceptance of love." During my journey on the *love bus*, I had to unlearn a lot of beliefs, and in the process of accepting myself in love, I found the gift of colour.

I had received the "download" about the *love* part of my *roadmap* in 1994, but as the saying goes, God gives food to every bird, but does not bring it to the nest. I had done research on living love for two years, and although I thought I was living love, I still had a long way to go. It is my belief that when someone close to you dies, they leave you a gift, but it is up to you to find the gift. When my mother died in 1996, she left me many gifts. After her death, many avenues opened for me to practice really living love. I started to practice yoga and was introduced to the energy centres, or chakras as they are known. Every centre corresponds to a colour and a specific musical note. During this time I met Penni du Plessis, who became my *colour teacher* and a lifelong friend.

My journey with colour started out as a hobby, but soon I became so passionate about the healing power of colour that I incorporated it into my own business as a healing modality, combining it with my own *ME* roadmap. I like to say that colour and your soul cannot lie.

Over the years, I have been able, with the grace of Spirit, to serve many people on their rainbow journeys by sharing my knowledge and love with them.

In 1996, the idea that colour could heal was in many circles laughed at. Twenty years later, I still find the same disbelief and scepticism in some circles. The only difference is I have experienced personally and in my healing practice over the years how powerful colour healing can be. I have made the commitment to myself to use my knowledge to heal myself spiritually, emotionally, and physically, and to help people who are attracted to colour healing. Every person in this world is influenced by colour every day. People often ask me, "What is Colour Healing Therapy?" Colour therapy joins the energy of light and the colour spectrum to assist in repairing the emotional imbalance that can create physical disharmony.

Colour works through and in us in every cell, nerve, gland, and muscle, and it shines in our auras and radiates upon us from the atmosphere. In our higher bodies, colour is an active power, exerting a tremendous influence in us on many levels.

The amazing power of colour was used in the Healing Temples of Light and Colour at Eliopoulos in Egypt and in ancient Greece, China, and India. We are simply remembering the healing and balancing power of colour that was used in the past — using it in a form that works for us right now. Every tool possible is needed to help the earth and the people on it to take responsibility for their own healing.

More and more people are becoming aware of energy or vibrational healing today. Homeopathy, reiki, yoga, colour healing, reflexology, and many other modalities combine the entire spectrum of healing possibilities using natural elements like colour, light, crystals, plants, heat, and sound to nourish the human energy system and aid the body in repairing its own balance of health. In this natural way, consciousness (awareness) is awakened and the body heals.

True healing is only complete when the cause of the condition or illness is addressed and transformed. In most cases, emotional pain or trauma of some sort, which is ignored, eventually manifests in a physical ailment. Most allopathic healing only looks at the physical imbalance. If not addressed, that which brought about the need for healing in the first place will resurface and manifest itself within the body in one form or another.

"When you make a solid commitment to restructure the spiritual vitality in yourself, there is no end to the healing that you can experience in all areas of your life."
— Sereda Aleta Dailey

The use of vibrational medicine creates a subtle energy stimulus that interacts with the energy system of the human body and helps to stabilise it on many different levels. By providing the correct focus of energy to the affected area, it begins to correct the balance. Once balance is restored, we can more effectively rid ourselves of toxins and negative patterns inhibiting our lives. Not only is vibrational medicine effective in healing, but also in stimulating deeper levels of consciousness.

Unfortunately, we do not give attention to imbalances in our body until we get physically sick. The habits we form through our thoughts, feelings, words, and actions can cause the body's energy centres to become weak, frozen, or blocked. Especially with all the demands and stress in our lives today, we have to learn to keep our energy on a high vibrational level. As Jim Rohn said, "Take care of your body. It's the only place you have to live."

Experiencing sickness is sometimes the only way we will stop and listen to our bodies, and I believe every discomfort in the body teaches us a lesson on an emotional and spiritual level. We never know how much we use all the parts of our body unless something goes wrong. Sickness, therefore, should be seen as a lesson teaching us gratitude and respect for our bodies and awareness of our thoughts and words. Working with my own illnesses through the years, I have found that the body heals when I heal on an emotional or spiritual level.

Write Your Story:
•   Write a few lines on how sickness was your teacher on a spiritual and emotional level.

Seeing In Colour As A Child
How much attention do you give to the colours surrounding you?

The chakra card in Jasmine Safi's Rainbow Cards says: "The colours of the universe live within you. Radiate their brilliance through the activation and healing of your chakras."

Many years ago, I met a retired reverend in his eighties. While we were talking, I asked him to tell me about his ability to see colour. He said as children who grew up on a farm and had no or very few toys, he and his friends played with the bones of the cattle that were slaughtered on the farm. He could see the bones in colour and would often ask his little friends to hand him his red cow, which they could not understand. It took him some time to understand that they could not see the colour in bones. To them, they were only playing with white bones, pretending they were their cattle.

Since this man was living with his daughter who made wedding dresses, I asked him whether he could see a difference in the colours surrounding the brides when they came to see his daughter and when they left. His answer was, "Yes, their colours are often angry or frustrated when they get here, but very relaxed and happy when they leave."

That made me realise that just because many people cannot see auras or colour does not mean they are not there. I spent a wonderful time with this interesting man who grew up in a time when colour healing was not known, and he would definitely have been reprimanded by his friends and family, in particular, the church authorities of the time, if they knew about his ability. The words of Ralph Waldo Emerson came to me as I left this amazing man: "Nature always wears the colours of the spirit." I often wonder why it is that we have so much trouble believing there is a whole world surrounding us we cannot hear, see, or touch. Just because we cannot see them does not mean there is no God or a Higher Intelligence or Energy.

Write Your Story:

- Did you have a special gift as a child you could not share with your friends out of fear you would be chastised, and can you let go of that fear on the *love bus*?

Getting Colour

> *"Never deprive someone of hope; it might be all they have."*
> — H. Jackson Brown, Jr

Have you gone through hard times when it felt as if you had no colour (fun) in your life?

I remember when I started working with colour in 1996, one of the first colours I worked with was pearl oil. The therapist who did the reading for me and introduced me to colour said, "You have a well of unshed tears inside you, and if you can heal your heart from all the sadness, you can achieve anything you want because you will be clearly guided by the Divine." In my personal healing journey, the words of Louise Hay were very appropriate: "You have the power to heal yourself, and you need to know that. We think so often that we are helpless, but we're not. We always have the power of our minds. Claim and consciously use your power."

Write Your Story:

- Write a few lines on your favourite colour or the colours you always choose and how you feel when you wear those colours.

Colouring Me (My Energy) With Rainbow Thoughts

"The soul becomes dyed with the colours of its thoughts."
— Marcus Aurelius

Do you choose to work with the positive of the colour of your thoughts? I have observed that many people starting their journey and learning about the meaning of colour will quickly tell me I am wearing a certain colour for the challenging or negative aspect of it. To be aware of what colour means does not necessarily mean that you know why the person is wearing the colour.

A few years ago, I was going through tremendous changes. I was aware of the challenging aspect of violet and that I was struggling with sadness and grief because of the changes coming to me. I knew I had to leave South Africa, but I did not know how it would happen or if it was forever. Every person who has immigrated can relate to the sadness they have to deal with. It is not only about leaving friends and family, but also your country of birth. After I arrived in New Zealand, I used orange for a long time to help me heal the shock of leaving and also for adapting in a new country. Yellow was used to bring sunshine and laughter into my life and negate the paralysing fears I had to deal with.

Write Your Story:

• Write a few lines about how you have dealt with difficult circumstances to bring the colour back into your life.

Playing On The Rays Of The Rainbow

"Healers are spiritual warriors who have found the courage to defeat the darkness of their souls. Awakening and rising from the depths of their deepest fears, like a Phoenix rising from the ashes. Reborn with a wisdom and strength that creates a light that shines bright enough to help, encourage, and inspire others out of their own darkness."
— Melanie Koulouris

Are you willing to become a *Rainbow Warrior*?

Through the years, I have written a few stories for my grandchildren about the *Rainbow Train*. I would like to show you the *Rainbow Train* with its interesting *Rainbow Passengers* in various stages of spiritual awakening. There is the carriage for the *Rainbow Babies*, those who are not even aware yet they are scared and driven by fear. They rush through life and blame everything and everybody for the problems in their lives. Like little children, they blindly lash out when they are angry.

Rainbow Teens are people who start to question life, the way they were brought up, their religion, and sometimes their very existence. They start to wake up and see they can change their lives by changing their way of thinking. They can be the ones who rebel against society's rules in trying to find new ways to love themselves.

As they grow in understanding on their journey through life, mostly when they go through some trauma, they can rightly be called the *Rainbow Seekers*. *Rainbow Seekers* are exploring avenues to better their lives. They may still blame the outside world for all that is wrong, but they are waking up to take responsibility for their own lives.

There is a colourful carriage for the *Rainbow Chasers*, who try to balance the madness called life; these are men and women rushing to work and meetings, who study to equip themselves better for their future and try to provide for their children on physical, emotional, and spiritual levels. They are trying to find time for their partners and are making a contribution in society by putting their various talents to use. In spite of all the demands, they bravely struggle on. They are the main part of any society, and I offer them a special seat on the *Rainbow Train*. They are our sons and daughters, the parents of our grandchildren. It is their responsibility to bring up tomorrow's leaders and to steer a country in the right direction. I am calling them the *Rainbow Chasers*.

In the next carriage are the *Rainbow Warriors*. They have weathered many storms and have an inner peace, knowing the strength of their inner light and power. They can calm a group with a word or just by their presence. People look up to them for their wisdom — they are the teachers and sages of the generations. *Rainbow Warriors* live amongst us quietly and steadfastly leading by their example.

Rainbow Weavers are the people who have learnt to live with grace, in gratitude, and joy under all circumstances. They weave the challenges and the blessings of every colour coming to them into a beautiful rainbow kite they can fly to colour their days with rainbow colours because they are radiating the right kind of energy to create their *Rainbow Days!*

A *Rainbow Catcher* is a *Rainbow Warrior*, like all of us — someone chasing life and happiness, but they mostly choose to play on the rainbow — and through their loving actions, they fly beautiful kites for fun — their own and others.

In South Africa, I knew two *Rainbow Catchers* who stood on the pavement in front of their houses every morning at peak hour. All they did was wave to people on their way to work. Imagine getting up in the morning, in the cold of winter, getting dressed, and walking out to stand there for half an hour or longer to wave to people and change their ordinary day into a *rainbow day*. One morning during the 2010 FIFA World Cup in South Africa, one of my *Rainbow Chasers* had a soccer hat on with all kinds of paraphernalia and a little flag he used to literally paint rainbows by waving to everybody. A businessman asked me when I related this story: "Why would anybody do that?" My answer was: "To brighten other people's day by making them smile while having fun themselves."

Warriors like that inspire you on your way to work to catch and hold your own rainbow for the day. I knew which days my *Rainbow Catchers* would be on their posts, so I would travel a different route to work on those days to see them and wave to them. I stopped one morning and handed them the story I had written about them. One of my *Warriors* was very humble and suddenly shy, but I knew he was all "pink" on the inside, appreciating my gratitude. The other *Warrior* said he would keep my story close to his heart for the rest of the day, bathing in that love. They were not young anymore, and I missed them when they were no longer standing on their corners. They taught me that you can fly your *Rainbow Kite* anywhere, even on a busy street, making *Rainbows* for lots of people on their way to work.

The *Rainbow Keepers* are the gurus of life. They are wise souls who make a difference in peoples' lives by living love unconditionally. They teach thousands of people the world over with their inspiring lives, speeches, and books. They have a magic surrounding them. I have a few *Rainbow Keepers* on my train. They have no specific carriage on the *Rainbow Train*, but move from one carriage to the next. Without doing anything special, they touch people's lives just by being on the *Rainbow Train*.

I invite you to choose a carriage and hop onto the *Rainbow Train*. The tickets are the lessons of life we all bring with us. Enjoy the ride!

Write Your Story:

• Write a few lines about the carriage you would like to join.

A Rainbow Gift for Your Journey

Have you tried writing about your friends and situations in colour?

I type in black, but I write in colour.

Reaching the end of my chapter about the important role colour is playing in my life and the lives of many other people, I would like to give you some of the rainbow colours to use to paint rainbows in your own life:

Red: A red spark will remind you that your energy can make anything work. It will inspire you with enthusiasm for life.

Orange: Orange is the colour to ignite your passion and for creating abundance on all levels.

Yellow: Take some yellow for joy, laughter, and loads of confidence. If fear comes knocking on your door, take out the yellow ray and dance away into a life of happiness.

Green: I give you a generous piece out of the green ray on the rainbow. It is to restore and renew your life. Green is the colour for growth and opening your heart to love.

Blue: The blue ray I hand to you for peaceful communication, to protect you, and for you to have faith and trust in yourself and others.

Indigo: Take a splash of indigo for clarity of thought and trusting your intuitive abilities.

Violet: Surround yourself with the soft violet beam in your meditations, and feel your energy being restored by connecting with your divine spark. Your rainbow cannot be without violet.

No life can escape transformation, sadness, and grief. It is our trump card through which we get confirmation of our faith in God.

I tie my gift of rainbow colours for you with *silver* and *gold* rays. May we form a network of silver light spreading our magnificent rainbows over the world and touching the lives of many people, showering them with the gold from our own hearts — giving love and receiving love in fulfilling our life's purpose.

Wishing you rainbow colours on your life's journey. My love enfolds you all.

Write Your Story:

- Are you ready to walk over your rainbow bridge, where life's lessons are hidden, and as a *Rainbow Warrior* sprinkle your gold dust over the world? What are you going to write in colour for the people in your world?

Summary

We can all spread divine rainbow colours using our words and deeds to paint on the canvas of our lives.

Healing our spirit and our emotions will heal the body. Illness is a lesson, teaching us to heal our lives through forgiveness and gratitude.

We all have special gifts, and it is our duty to develop and use them. Our thoughts colour our whole world. We are all *Rainbow Warriors* chasing happiness, peace, and the wonder of life that is love.

The Biggest Lessons

Colour has a language of its own. The choices of your soul and colour never lie.

Word Reveal And The Power Of Words

Word reveal for Rainbow: rain, bow, I, in, won, win, brain, and brow, to name a few. Looking at the meanings of bow, it can mean a knot tied with two loops and two loose ends, used for decorative ribbons. It can also be a weapon for shooting arrows. I made the following power sentence:

Seeing my chakras as my inner colourful *bow* and my feet and head as the loose ends to expand into Mother Earth and the Sky, I become an *archer (Ace)*, shooting my arrows of love from my rainbow — painting my world rainbow.

Rainbow Blessing

May the healing rays of the rainbow bless your life every day with their power.

"Colours speak all languages."
— Joseph Addison

Chapter 20 — Finding Your Pot Of Gold

Your Pot — Your Choice

"When you are inspired…dormant forces, faculties, and talents become alive, and you discover yourself to be a greater person by far than you ever dreamed yourself to be."

— Patanjali

All through Chapter 19, I took you on the *Rainbow Train*, trying to show you how the colours surrounding us and the colours of our thoughts, emotions, and words colour our lives. In this last chapter, together we will find the inspiration for our life's love journeys in the pot of gold.

Throughout this book, I have tried to inspire and ignite the flame within you. Now the choice is yours. Write your own script for life. You have the power to say, "This is not how my story will end." You can rewrite your story to become the best love story ever, which will result in you "living happily ever after."

"Truth, like gold, is to be obtained not by its growth, but by washing away from it all that is not gold."

— Leo Tolstoy

Do you know we all have a pot of gold within us? The quote above is true if we start to see ourselves as the pot of gold, and instead of trying to grow into someone other than what we are, start to unlearn all the lies we live with and find our own truth.

One of the young rainbow children coming to me for healing told me a beautiful lesson during one of our sessions. I was telling him about the rainbow and how he can play on the rainbow to help with his healing. He was a very wise eleven-year old when he came to me for therapy. Listening intently to my explanation, he suddenly said, with a very serious look on his face, "You know there is not really a pot of gold at the end of the rainbow. I know because there was a rainbow at our school once, and when we looked at the end, there was nothing."

For a moment, I was without words. I looked at him, wondering how Spirit was going to get me out of this dilemma, when he suddenly said with a light in his eyes, "Oh, now I understand. If we play on the rainbow, which is inside us, and get to the end, it means we are the pot of gold because we find ourselves!"

How easy it is for children to accept colour and that they are the pot of gold. Balancing ME (my energy) and living love means I am the pot of gold. Whenever I see the letter "L" in a word, I always read it as "love." Taking away the "L" in gold", we have the answer: God. I have said it does not matter what you call the Higher Powers above us, next to us, behind us, or in front of us, and most of all within us. Another word in Gold is glo(w). Sprinkling gold dust around us and into our world with a love anchored in God can make our whole world glo!

I agree with Carlos Barrios when he said, "The greatest wisdom is in simplicity, love, respect, tolerance, sharing, gratitude, forgiveness. It's not complex or elaborate. The real knowledge is free. It's encoded in your DNA. All you need is within you. Great teachers have said that from the beginning. Find your heart, and you will find your way."

Write Your Story:

- Write your story about how you plan to share your gold, which we can say is God within. Living love, we can create our Heaven on Earth. (Our Heaven in our heart.)

Being A Teacher Means Serving Humanity

Some people are teachers without knowing it. What is a teacher? He or she is like a well filled with wisdom. What is a well? It is a deep pit filled with water and the place where we always feel welcome. You have a choice at the well. You can quench your thirst and walk away. Or you can sit there and rest for a while. You can take some of the wealth with you, or you can get into that well and, for a while, be immersed in the full strength of it. Sai Baba was one of my teachers in life who, without ever meeting him in person, was a *well* where I could sit and drink from the pure water of his wisdom. He said, "Teach your children about truth, right conduct, peace, love and non-violence. Then they can go into any religion in the world, for that is the basis of all religions."

All my wonderful teachers had certain characteristics in common. They had self-discipline, continually did self-study, and knew that we create our world from the inside. Gratitude and happiness was their way of living love. They radiated energy of pureness and lived with an unwavering faith in a Higher Power. Marianne Williamson, in her book, *A Return to Love*, says:

> Our Deepest Fear is not that we are inadequate. Our deepest fear is that we are powerful beyond measure. It is our light, not our darkness, that most frightens us. We ask ourselves: Who am I to be brilliant, gorgeous, talented, and fabulous? Actually, who are you not to be? You are a child of God. You playing small doesn't serve the world. There's nothing enlightened about shrinking so that other people won't feel insecure around you. We were born to make manifest the Glory of God that is within us. It is not just in some of us; it is in everyone. And, as we let our own light shine, we unconsciously give other people permission to do the same. As we are liberated from our fear, our presence automatically liberates others.

Write Your Story:
- Have you got a Divine teacher whom you carry in your heart?

Being "ME" Means Constantly Being In "I Am"

"The words I am, which you consistently use to define who you are and what you are capable of, are holy expressions for the name of God — the highest aspect of yourself."
— Dr Wayne Dyer

I am the pot of gold. I am a miracle. These sentences should be written in our diaries and on our mirrors to remind us daily of *who* we really are. It would not matter if we were a CEO of a multimillion dollar company, or a person without identity and a proper job, when we acknowledge the essence of ME (my energy), we will treat every living thing *right*, be *fit* to handle our lessons, and shine our *light* into the world. I have not yet found a person who does not have to deal with fear and love on a daily basis. Even the enlightened souls have their daily dose of fear lessons. The only difference is when we know we have a choice, it makes it easier and much quicker to bounce back into the pot of gold. Sai Baba said: "Life is a challenge; meet it! Life is a dream; realise it! Life is a game; play it! Life is *Love*; enjoy it!"

Write Your Story:

• How are you going to remind yourself you are God's miracle?

The Rainbow Circle, Angels, Anchors, And ME

"The cave you fear to enter holds the treasure you seek."
— Joseph Campbell

Are you prepared to live in the moment?

I have written about my experiences with excellence, and that the word for me means to be constantly aware of how to outgrow my own dead or frozen cells. It means finding better ways to keep my mind occupied than allowing fear thoughts to contaminate my mind and my body. Lao Tzu said it in such a beautiful way: "If you want to awaken all of humanity, awaken all of yourself. If you want to eliminate the suffering in the world, then eliminate all that is dark and negative in yourself. Truly, the greatest gift you have to give is that of your own self-transformation." I cannot say I meditate at certain times, but for years, I have been in walking, talking meditation with Spirit. I speak to the Spirit of my soul many times throughout the day, almost like a child with an imaginary friend. My grandson once asked me why I talk to myself. I answered, "I am talking to Spirit. It is almost like talking to yourself, but you have to listen intently to hear the answer."

Special times are in the evenings, when I am preparing my mind for sleep, and in the mornings, when I wake up. Every morning, my heart rejoices to meet another day. Recently, I was going into my "sleep meditative state" and found myself walking into a beautiful cave. I was standing inside an amethyst geode. I looked around, filled with wonder, and realised I was taken on a rainbow journey about my own life. I weaved the sadness and grief of my life into the beauty of sitting in this cave with my *Guardian Angel*, rejoicing in awe at my own transformation. Standing in that beautiful cave, I felt as if I were standing in the doorway to a cosmic world where I could experience the peace and wisdom of being one with God. It was as if I were going through a cleansing of my energy field, and a circle of protective light was about me like a soft, warm indigo cloak, emitting beautiful silver with light violet and dark purple sparks shining like stars. I know violet is the colour of transformation, of beginnings and endings. I was looking into my soul, seeing with clarity the effects of my decisions.

As I slowly walked through the cave, it changed into the most beautiful golden yellow. Looking closely at the walls and the roof, I realised I had entered a part of the cave made out of amber. Momentarily, I was stunned by the beauty surrounding me. It was almost more beautiful than the first part of the cave. I looked back over my journey and realised gold was used to heal and balance my life force. Due to my experiences earlier on my life's journey, I shut down my intuition, or my gut feelings, because they could not be explained in a linear world. The repression of my gifts as a healer caused my emotional body to get out of balance, manifesting as deep depression. I looked on as if I were a spectator, seeing myself struggling in the pit of despair and then walking that lonely road in the desert. What I experienced as fear and god forsakenness, or as sand and dry desert in a burning sun, were these beautiful amber-gold and yellow colours assisting me in removing the obstacles I had placed in my own way. I saw myself being healed physically as I was healed of negative energies on an emotional level. As my energy frequencies rose to higher vibrations, I had the courage to start living my life's purpose. I found my own power and wisdom through my experiences. I learnt to go with the flow of life with grace, contentment, and cheerfulness, but also with devotion and commitment to my path. Ultimately, I saw, as if looking through a mirror onto my own past, the golden rope of spiritual support showering me with the gold of God's Love. Through this golden cord, I connected my energy to Light Beings on Earth and to helping people understand our experiences are there to serve us. We learn to weave the good and the bad of our own lives into beautiful rainbows that "glo" with golden love.

I moved out of that part of the cave. Suddenly, I found myself at the end of the tunnel, and I walked out into a forest bathed in moonlight. Spellbound, I looked at the beauty of nature and listened to the breeze in the trees with deep peace and quiet all around me. I was sitting in the energy of my heart, enjoying the union with higher realms. I had come full circle on my *Rainbow Journey*. In humility and with gratitude, I could feel the energy of the Universe flowing through me, infusing me with the strength to take my rightful place in the world and to remember in my earthly body I can help to bring love and light into the physical world. The light anchoring me to the angels and the Divine were all around me like light beams. Clarity surrounded me like a silver cloak. Floating on the light beams into my heart was this message: "Learn to love your prison and it becomes your shelter and your friend." I smiled. For the first time, I understood "atonement." When you accept yourself, you are "ME at one" or "a team."

I slept surrounded by the wonder of it all, knowing freedom is hiding in all of us. When our hearts and minds are in tune, we are free and no-thing or no-one can imprison us.

Write Your Story:

- Have you gone into the cave where your Rainbow journey started and found you have come full circle?
- Did you meet your Angels who are keeping your Energy firmly anchored in this wonderful university of Earth and teaching you about the love in your heart?

Thank you for coming on this journey with me. I have travelled this road for many years. It is a trip worth taking. Remember, when your life falls apart, out of the dark night of your soul can be born a new awareness and a life showered with blessings.

I would like to end this book with a reminder from Ufuoma Apoki to you: "The beauty about gold, though, is that in all states from uncertainty to conviction it never for once gives up its lustre." It does not matter where you are on your *Rainbow Journey*; all you have to remember is you already have a *light* within. It is up to you how much you want to clean the *light* to see the *golden lustre*.

I leave you with "Goodbye", which in the days when it was first used, was meant as a blessing, "God be with ye."

Then God said: "It is done."

Summary

We may not always have control over our circumstances, but we can always choose our attitude. Accepting we are the pot of gold means we acknowledge and accept God lives within us, and we can spread the message of love all over the world.

Great teachers spread love by serving humanity in some way. Freedom is not to be found on the outside. When our minds and hearts are in tune, we are free and no-thing or no-one can imprison us.

The Biggest Lessons

Freedom always hides inside our minds. Finding our inner rainbow means finding we are the pot of gold.

Word Reveal And The Power Of Words

The word reveal of *atonement* makes the phrase ME at one or a team. As a last power sentence, I would like to leave you with this thought: Don't let fear steal your joy and the glory of your greatness.

Rainbow Blessing

May your *Rainbow Journey* lead you to happiness. I am waiting for you on the sunny side of the clouds.

A Final Note
— Acting as the Ace You were Born to Be

"God is the ultimate experience of silence, of beauty, of bliss,
a state of inner celebrations."

— Rajneesh

This is the moment where I like saying to delegates attending my courses you can get motivated through a course or a book. Tomorrow, you have to go back to work and face your reality. As you were reading through this book, I hope you completed the parts where you could write your story. I encourage you to read through your story and see how far you have come since you started reading my book. Do you have clarity as to how you are going to implement changes or keep the momentum to carry on living a life filled with love? In the Preface of this book, I gave you the basis for the Rainbow Roadmap namely, ME=EM: *"The impact of My Energy is determined by my choices and how much effort I put into my Energy Management."* In Chapter 18, I wrote that I even sign my name to people who know me well as Meem to remind me about the value of these four letters for me.

This book has given you a roadmap, one I still use every day. The choice is yours. Are you going to put this book on the shelf or start to apply the roadmap and the techniques? I would like to challenge you to act. It is good to start with what you think, feel, and say right now. Experience the feelings even if they are very negative, and if you experience that feeling in the silence of your heart, you will find the answer to grow into love. I recently worked with the word and the feeling of being *overwhelmed*. Working with my feeling and unravelling the word, I realised I had to *redeem ME* (my energy) and *move* towards *love*. Finding the right word and acting on that, the feeling of being overwhelmed was gone. When you experience fear in any way, know that your energy is struggling to get you back to love.

Depending on your reactions to fear, you can start with a word you often repeat or you can start with a feeling you have. If you start with a word, feel how you feel when you say the word and what is the thought behind your word. Starting with a feeling you have, find a word and then the thought behind your feeling. The last time in your own book write your feeling, word and thought, and work towards the word or the feeling of love you would like to experience. Trust your heart; you will know when you are taking the right action because you will feel lighter. Repeat your exercise until you feel you can see the results of living on the love side of your bus.

In this book you learnt how our thoughts, feelings, and words influence our actions on all levels. You assessed your fear reactions. You learnt to *face* your *fears* and what we often see as *facts* can be our perceptions but not the truth.

We had *fun* with all the words revealed to us, and I am sure you are more aware now how to find the truth and the power within a word.

I hope during this journey, you found many *facets* of yourself and also acknowledged the beauty within you. You now have the knowledge to look at your life with the understanding everything is energy and your thoughts and words have higher energy vibrations when you practice gratitude, joy, and love, which contribute to healthy minds and bodies. The healing power of colour that surrounds us daily can be used in many ways to heal energetically.

Working through the book and writing your own story, you had the chance to break free from outdated beliefs.

If you work with the techniques I have offered, you will find your own *Divinely Coloured Rainbow*. Changing the way we think and practising the power of high vibrational words, together with the healing power of colour, are keys available in this book for finding love. I challenge you with a quote from Aberjhani: "Dare to love yourself as if you were a rainbow with gold at both ends." As you read through the notes you made in your book, please feel free to share with me about your journey and how you are planning to continue living love. It will be my pleasure and a privilege to hear from you about how much this book has helped you to get rid of your fears and to live the love you deserve. You can find my contact information in the back of the book.

I wish you abundance on all levels of your life! May your *Rainbow Kites* fly high!

Rainbow Blessings.

Jansie Bond

"Your words have power. Speak words that are kind, loving, positive, uplifting, encouraging, and life-giving."
— Author Unknown

About the Author

Jansie Bond is a self-discovery facilitator, colour therapist, yoga teacher, and author. She believes everybody has a fire or a light within and igniting that flame can start their own healing from emotional challenges, which causes them to live in fear. She inspires and motivates people to take responsibility for their own wellbeing by using the *roadmap* she and many of her fellow Rainbow travellers follow on a daily basis. Many people have found their truth and healed their lives through her workshops and courses.

Jansie grew up in a farming community in South Africa where everybody spoke Afrikaans. Words fascinated her from a young age, and even before she could write, she would ask her mom to write down her poems. To strengthen her English-speaking abilities, she decided to only read English books. After completing college, she married and lived in Pretoria, South Africa, for forty years until emigrating to Wellington, New Zealand, in 2013. She and her husband moved again in 2021 during the Covid-19 pandemic to the Gold Coast, Australia, to be closer to their children and grandchildren.

Jansie Bond is your ordinary wife, mom, and grandmother. For many years, she stayed at home supporting her husband and being a full-time mom for their two children. The family home was always open to anyone who needed an ear to listen, a warm hug, or a hot meal.

Jansie spread her wings when the children went their own ways. Working as a real estate agent, her entrepreneurial spirit led to further studies and becoming the principal of her own real estate business. Through studying and reading many self-development, motivational, and inspirational books on self-healing, Jansie developed her own *roadmap* to overcome depression and realised her calling was in the healing field. While pursuing her life purpose as a self-discovery facilitator, colour therapist, and yoga teacher, she never fails to make time for gardening, enjoying her special bond with plants and animals.

In her self-discovery business, she inspires others to take responsibility for their own health and healing. Over the past twenty-five years, she has helped many people in private sessions and through her workshops and courses, also in the corporate world — to understand fear and love motivation. Being aware of the effects of fear and love in their daily lives, people can make choices to create a culture of love where everybody can excel as a champion. Using the renewed appreciation for the power of their thoughts, feelings, words and actions they can use trust, honesty and strong moral principles as cornerstones for themselves and their workplaces.

Through self-discovery, Jansie has helped people with relationship problems, depression, addictions, and many other emotional and physical ailments; she teaches we become what we think, feel, and say and our physical body is the instrument by which we can measure our spiritual and emotional wellbeing. The body's cell memory retains everything that happens to us emotionally and spiritually. She believes in healing massages "because the body is the last place where we let go of trauma and pain."

Living her life according to the principles, knowledge, experiences, and wisdom she has accumulated over a lifetime, she wrote her book *Fear and Love Motivation* while rebuilding her business in New Zealand.

Moving to Australia and adapting once again in a new country took all her skills to bring back balance into her life. It is with great excitement and gratitude towards her publisher that she is preparing the second edition of her book for publishing in print and eBook formats.

Rainbow Divinity Courses, Workshops, and Individual Coaching

Jansie Bond developed her "Rainbow Roadmap" to heal herself from depression. The *roadmap* teaches how we create our world with our thoughts, feelings, words, and actions.

When you work with Jansie, you will find yourself surrounded by a safe and trusting space during the workshops and therapies. There you will come to understand that facing your fear and working with fear instead of living with shame, blame, or guilt can be the starting point for healing yourself. The training is aimed at helping you change your fear-based life of pain and struggle into a life motivated by love — with an increased chance to live a life of gratitude, happiness, and abundance — and passing those positive attributes on to the people you interact with in both your private and public lives. Changing how and what we think, feel, and say is a journey that will take you to achieving your highest potential.

Jansie's extensive knowledge and experience about the healing power of colour therapy is used to enhance her therapies and workshops. Rainbow Divinity's "Roadmap" is closely interwoven with the healing power of colour. Learning the language of colour and understanding the messages of your colour choices will increase your self-awareness. Learning to use colour to support yourself and others in all areas of your life can open you up to a world of peace and joy, instead of staying stuck in the challenges of a fear-filled life.

Training and Individual Sessions offered by Jansie

Jansie has travelled her "Rainbow Journey" for many years and have been immensely blessed to see how people changed their lives through her workshops and individual coaching sessions. She believes our purpose on Earth is to offer our service with love to benefit the Earth and all who dwell on her. Jansie is excited and rejoices with every client who ignites the fire of love within themselves and becomes a light beacon in their personal and work environment.

ME (My Energy) Workshops

This two-day course is the "flagship" training of Rainbow Divinity. It can also be scheduled over a longer period with a series of shorter workshops to give delegates time to really change their patterns of behaviour and build a strong foundation to change their lives from fear-based to love-based.

During this course, you will discover how you react when facing stressful situations and how to find the answers for your fear reactions in your thoughts, feelings, words, and actions. You will be introduced to "Rainbow Language" and techniques so you can start working with your fear and change behaviour patterns to become "fit" to handle emotional pressures.

Understanding many of our perceptions can be misleading, and learning to be aware of the energy of our thoughts, feelings, words, and actions takes us into a space where it is easier to find happiness and health instead of getting caught up in fearful debilitating behaviour.

While working with your fears, you learn about forgiveness, finding self-acceptance, and self-love. You rediscover your spiritual calling for being here on Earth. You reconnect with gratitude for the gift of life. You understand the flame of love inside you can never be extinguished through any evil you experienced. If you choose to allow challenges you experience to be your "roadmap", you will be led back to the love within you.

The "**Energy Management**" workshops are also taught in the corporate domain. Fear influences employee turnover, sick leave, and productivity, directly impacting the financial side of companies. Increasing self-esteem and self-respect of individuals with a culture of Excellence through eradicating bullying, blame, and guilt results in the wellbeing of a whole company.

Healing herself from depression was only the beginning of Jansie's colourful journey of meeting wonderful people and receiving many blessings along the way. Applying these principles helped many other people change their lives from emotional and physical sickness to living in the constant flow of wellbeing.

The Language of Colour

We are all surrounded by colour every day. This four-day course teaches the positive and challenging aspect of every colour's physical, emotional, and mental symptoms, and the meaning of choosing a colour in the specific ranges. Practical training is paramount in application of the various options for how to use colour as a healing technique. With the unique language of your colour choices, you can introduce a gentle process of healing imbalances in your body — letting go of pain and trauma and finding happiness within yourself. The wonderful process of colour healing can successfully be incorporated with many other healing modalities, enhancing existing wellness businesses.

Stay in Contact

Rainbow Divinity workshops and courses, together with individual healing sessions, are listed on Jansie's Facebook page. All the workshops and courses can be adapted to company and employee needs. Tell Jansie about you, your challenges, and your fear situations. She would like to chat with you on Zoom, WhatsApp, or in person to assist you on your Journey.

Contact Jansie Bond:

https://www.facebook.com/RainbowDivinity/

Email: jansiebond@gmail.com

www.ingramcontent.com/pod-product-compliance
Lightning Source LLC
Chambersburg PA
CBHW061154120626
46546CB00005B/2054